TABLE OF CONTENTS

Harriet Tubman

History Maker Bios

Maryann N. Weidt

LER█ █EAPOLIS

To *Pearl Belton*
(and the Visible Woman)

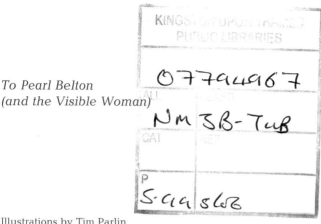
Illustrations by Tim Parlin

Text copyright © 2003 by Maryann N. Weidt
Illustrations copyright © 2003 by Lerner Publications Company

Lerner Publications Company
A division of Lerner Publishing Group
241 First Avenue North
Minneapolis, MN 55401 U.S.A.

Website address: www.lernerbooks.com

Library of Congress Cataloging-in-Publication Data

Weidt, Maryann N.
    Harriet Tubman / by Maryann N. Weidt.
        p.   cm. — (History maker bios)
    Includes bibliographical references (p.) and index.
    ISBN: 0–8225–4676–0 (lib. bdg. : alk. paper)
    1. Tubman, Harriet, 1820?–1913—Juvenile literature. 2. Slaves—United
States—Biography—Juvenile literature. 3. African American women—
Biography—Juvenile literature. 4. Underground railroad—Juvenile literature.
5. Antislavery movements—United States—History—19th century—Juvenile
literature. [1. Tubman, Harriet, 1820?–1913. 2. Slaves. 3. African Americans—
Biography. 4. Women—Biography. 5. Underground railroad.] I. Title. II. Series.
E444.T82 W45 2003
973.7'115—dc21   2002005527

Manufactured in the United States of America
1 2 3 4 5 6 – JR – 08 07 06 05 04 03

INTRODUCTION

Harriet Tubman worked on the Underground Railroad. This railroad had nothing to do with trains. It was a group of people like Harriet who helped slaves escape to freedom in the North in the 1800s.

Before Harriet saved other slaves, she was a slave herself. Even as a little girl, she worked very hard and was beaten often. In 1849, she escaped to Philadelphia, where slavery was illegal. Her angry master and people who wanted a reward searched for her. Still, Harriet made nineteen trips back into the dangerous South and rescued over three hundred slaves. She became famous as a person who was not afraid to risk her life to help others.

This is her story.

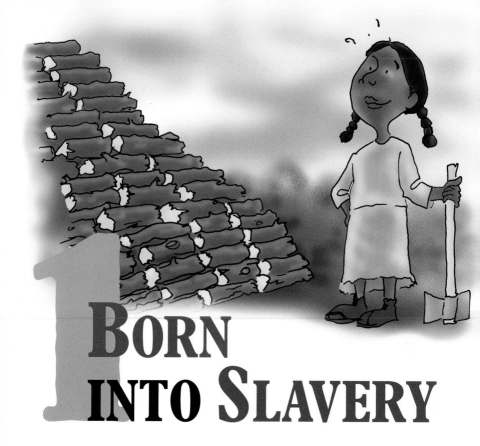

1 BORN INTO SLAVERY

By the time Harriet Ross was six years old, she knew all about hard work. She worked all day, almost every day, on a farm near Bucktown, Maryland. Harriet's mother and father were slaves. And right from the moment Harriet was born, in about 1820, she was a slave, too. So were her ten brothers and sisters. A white man owned them all.

One of the jobs Harriet had to do was check muskrat traps. She waded into an icy river to see if any animals had been caught. Her feet were bare and her shirt was thin. Once, when Harriet caught a fever from doing this cold, wet job, her master became angry. He thought she was faking her illness so she wouldn't have to work.

Soon, red spots appeared on her body. She had the measles. But the master wouldn't let Harriet's mother take care of her. Harriet's mother had to work in the fields, with the other slaves.

Most slaves had little free time for playing or relaxing. Even young children had to work almost every day.

Harriet lay alone on the floor of her family's one-room shack. She thought about the master's children. When they got sick, they stayed in a warm bed in a big house. Harriet wondered why her family had to live this way.

Harriet recovered from the measles, and she grew up strong. By the time she was ten years old, she worked in the fields with the adult slaves. She harvested wheat and husked corn. She drove an ox cart and plow. Sometimes she helped her father cut wood and haul logs. Everyone said she worked as hard as any man. In one day, she could cut a pile of wood four feet high.

Many planters, like the man who owned Harriet, lived in big, fancy houses.

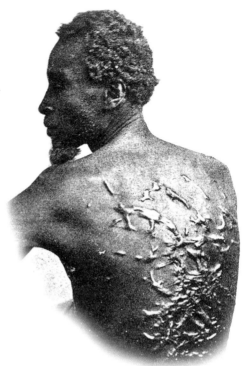

This slave's back was scarred from whippings.

Harriet worked from sunrise to sunset. A man called an overseer watched the slaves' every move, and he was cruel. He whipped the slaves if he thought they weren't working hard enough. Harriet's back was slashed with scars from the whip.

Sometimes, stories about a different kind of life in the North were whispered among the slaves. Harriet listened carefully. It was against the law to own slaves there. Black people were free. At night, Harriet dreamed about being free.

A master and his overseer (on horseback)

When Harriet was about fifteen, a slave named Jim sneaked away from the fields. The overseer noticed and chased after him with his whip. Harriet followed them both.

The overseer caught up to Jim at a store in town and began yelling at him. Jim bolted out the door and ran. The overseer ordered Harriet to stop him. Instead, Harriet stood in the door and blocked the overseer's path. The overseer was furious. He picked up a two-pound iron weight and threw it at Harriet. It struck her on the forehead, and she collapsed onto the floor, bleeding. Everyone thought she was dead.

Harriet wasn't dead, but she was barely alive. All that winter, she lay on the floor of her family's tiny shack. Her mother took care of her when she could. Other slaves looked in on her and wondered if she would survive. The overseer tried to sell her, but no one wanted a half-dead slave.

NOT SO SWEET

One day when Harriet was about seven years old, she noticed a bowl of sugar lumps on her master's kitchen table. Harriet had never tasted anything sweet. When she thought nobody was looking, she snatched one. But the master's wife caught her. To avoid a whipping, Harriet ran and hid in a pigpen. She stayed with the pigs for four days and nights, fighting them for potato scraps. Finally, she was so hungry that she went back to the house. When found, she was whipped twice: once for stealing the sugar and once for running away.

After a while, Harriet got better. But the injury had caused a problem. Harriet sometimes fell asleep suddenly—even if she was talking or working. Her master and overseers thought she was stupid. But they were wrong. Harriet noticed everything that went on around her. She noticed when slaves were whipped. She noticed when there wasn't enough food.

As Harriet grew older, she became angry that she was a slave. And she was angry that *anyone* could be a slave. She sometimes touched the deep scar on her forehead and thought of Jim running away. And she wondered, How would it feel to be free?

2 ESCAPE!

In 1844, Harriet married a man named John Tubman. John was a black man who had been born free. Harriet worked in the fields during the day and stayed with John in his cabin at night. She talked to him about running away, but he said she was foolish. He didn't understand why she would risk her life that way. Harriet decided to stay with John for the time being.

In 1849, something happened to change Harriet's mind. That year, her master died. Harriet heard that she and other slaves would be sold to a new master who lived farther south. As bad as it was to be a slave in Maryland, it was worse in the deep South. Life was much harsher on the cotton plantations there. Harriet knew what she had to do. She would run away after all, that very night. She didn't tell John. She didn't trust him to keep her secret.

Families were often broken up when slaves were sold to different masters. This illustration shows a mother being sold while her child is kept behind.

Desperate slaves tried many ways of escaping north. This man mailed himself to the free city of Philadelphia in a crate.

Harriet set out for freedom late at night. Two of her brothers came with her, but they soon became scared and wanted to go back. They knew that if they were caught, they would be punished severely. They might even be killed. Harriet wanted to go on without them, but they convinced her to go back, too. At home again, she climbed into bed with John. But she knew she would try again.

Two nights later, Harriet wrapped a piece of bread in a cloth. Then she was on her way—this time alone. She knew of a kind white woman who might help her, and she found the woman's house. The woman gave Harriet two pieces of paper with names on them. They were the names of families who would help her on her way north. These slips of paper were Harriet's first "tickets" on the Underground Railroad.

The woman who helped Harriet may have been a Quaker, like the people pictured here. Quakers were opposed to slavery and believed that everyone was equal in the eyes of God.

Although the Underground Railroad was not really underground, some people did dig tunnels under their homes to hide runaways there.

The Underground Railroad was not a real railroad. And it was not underground. It was a group of people who helped runaway slaves. People in one house, or "station," might offer a place to hide and a meal to eat. Then they would show the runaway, or "passenger," how to get to the next station. Sometimes a person acted as a guide for runaways. These people were called "conductors."

Harriet traveled only at night, when it was easier to avoid being seen. She ran through fields and forests. She trudged through swamps and heavy brush. During the day, she hid in haystacks or fields. Sometimes she went to a station on the Underground Railroad, and people hid her in a barn, cellar, or attic.

Harriet headed north along the Choptank River into Delaware. On clear nights, she followed the shimmering North Star. On cloudy nights, she checked the trees. Her father had taught her that moss grows on the north side of trees.

Runaway slaves usually traveled at night through swamps and forests, where it was easy to hide.

The free city of Philadelphia during the 1850s

After many days of walking, Harriet finally made it to the northern city of Philadelphia, Pennsylvania. At last she was free! No one in the North could be made a slave. No overseers could whip her. No one could tell her what to do or how to do it. Harriet looked down at her hands to see if she was the same person. She felt like she was in heaven.

Philadelphia was a big city, with horses and wagons cramming the streets. People shouted at one another. Peddlers sold hats, apples, and cooking pots. Harriet found a job in a hotel kitchen. She was pleased to finally be paid for her work.

Philadelphia was also lonely. There was no one to welcome Harriet to the free land. But before long she met people who were part of the Underground Railroad. Soon, they made a plan for Harriet to rescue her sister's family. It would be very dangerous. Her master would have people looking for Harriet to return her to slavery. To Harriet, it was worth the risk.

William Still was a part of the Underground Railroad in Philadelphia. He later published a book about all the slaves he helped escape.

Harriet Tubman, conductor on the Underground Railroad

In December of 1850, Harriet returned to Maryland. Again, she hid during the day. She hurried through woods and swamps at night. Soon she was guiding her sister and her sister's two children back north to freedom. Harriet had become a conductor on the Underground Railroad.

A few months later, Harriet decided to make the dangerous trip south again. This time she rescued her brother and two other men. After that, she made many more trips south. Soon, Harriet became well known as a hero. Slaves whispered to one another about her bravery. They called her Moses. In the Bible, Moses rescued his people from slavery. Now Harriet Tubman was doing what she could to rescue hers.

"Go On or Die"

Sometimes the people Harriet was rescuing became tired or scared. Sometimes they wanted to go back to their masters, or maybe just collapse where they were standing. Harriet knew that if any runaway gave up, Harriet and the other runaways would all be in danger. When a slave complained, Harriet pulled out a pistol she carried. "You'll go on or die," she said. After that, people always changed their minds. And Harriet always got them to freedom.

3 A PRICE ON HER HEAD

In 1850, a new law made Harriet's work much harder. It was called the Fugitive Slave Law. It said that anyone who found runaway slaves had to report them so they could be returned to their master. Even a freed slave in the Northern states could be returned to slavery. Disobeying the law meant a big fine, and maybe jail.

Now Harriet had to bring slaves all the way to Canada. The journey to freedom was longer and more dangerous than ever. Authorities along the way worked harder to capture escaped slaves. Large rewards were offered for the capture of runaways.

But the Underground Railroad worked harder, too. Harriet became one of its best conductors. She had no fear of being caught—it was much more important to fight against slavery. Harriet said God would keep her safe.

Harriet (FAR LEFT, WITH PAN) and some former slaves she had rescued

CHICKEN RUN

On one rescue mission, Harriet had to pass through Bucktown, Maryland. One of her former masters still lived nearby. Harriet pulled her sun hat down over her face in case she ran into him. She also bought a couple live chickens. When she saw her former master coming toward her, she dropped the chickens. They squawked and fluttered, and Harriet scrambled on the ground trying to catch the screaming birds. Harriet's plan worked! The man didn't recognize her because he saw only the top of her hat. And he didn't suspect a thing.

By 1856, Harriet had rescued so many slaves that slave masters knew who she was. They offered a reward of $40,000 for her arrest. Still, Harriet kept on bringing slaves out of the South. She even rescued her parents, who could barely walk. She bought a home in Auburn, New York, to share with them.

Frederick Douglass was a fierce abolitionist and a good friend of Harriet.

Many people in the United States and Europe believed slavery was wrong, and they were working to end it. These people were called abolitionists. Harriet began to give speeches at abolitionist meetings across the country. She used the money she earned from these speeches to help rescue more slaves.

Once, on her way to a meeting in Boston, Harriet stopped in Troy, New York. There she heard that a runaway slave had been captured. He was in the courthouse and was going to be sent back to his owner. Harriet had to do something.

Quickly, she gathered a crowd of her abolitionist friends. She told some young boys to yell "Fire!" and the crowd grew even larger. When the authorities removed the slave from the courthouse, Harriet grabbed onto his arm. She knocked down two men and dragged the slave away. A huge fight broke out in the crowd, but Harriet carried the man through. Finally, she put him in a boat.

This image was published in a pamphlet by a group called the Anti-Slavery Society.

AM I NOT A MAN AND A BROTHER?

The slave escaped, but he was captured again on the other side of the river. Harriet didn't give up—she rescued him once more. This time, she successfully brought him to Canada.

Harriet's daring courthouse rescue was an important victory for abolitionists. People everywhere heard about Harriet's fight against slavery. When Harriet arrived in Boston, she spoke to crowds all over the city. More and more people agreed with Harriet that slavery was wrong. And she was more determined than ever to end it.

4 WAR HERO

In 1860, Abraham Lincoln was elected president of the United States. Lincoln believed slavery was wrong. Slave owners in the South worried that Lincoln would outlaw slavery. They said they could not run their farms and plantations without slaves.

After Lincoln was elected, seven Southern states decided to break off from the United States and form their own country. More Southern states soon joined them. Lincoln told the states that they could not break off from the United States. In April of 1861, the Southern army attacked a U.S. fort in South Carolina. The Civil War had begun.

With a war going on, Harriet's friends convinced her to stop traveling into the South to rescue slaves. Harriet agreed. She had made nineteen trips into the Southern states. She had rescued over three hundred people from slavery. It was time to look for new ways to help.

Abraham Lincoln led the United States through the Civil War.

During the Civil War, many black people in the South packed everything they had into wagons and fled to the North.

In the spring of 1862, the Union (Northern) Army freed many slaves in South Carolina. Despite the dangers of the war, Harriet went there to help the former slaves. These people had almost nothing. Harriet used the little money she had to build a laundry. That way, black women could earn money by washing clothes for the Union soldiers. Harriet showed other former slaves how to make items to sell to the soldiers.

Harriet worked for the Union Army in other ways. If the soldiers were hungry, she tied on an apron and cooked. If the army needed a nurse, she used roots and herbs to heal sick and wounded men. Harriet scrubbed floors, and she swatted flies. She served her country by doing whatever needed to be done.

Both free blacks and former slaves joined the Union Army to fight against the South.

Harriet even worked as a spy. Because of her time on the Underground Railroad, she knew her way through forests and across fields. And slaves in the South trusted her and shared information with her. She sneaked into Southern army camps and learned what she could about the army's plans.

BLACK SOLDIERS

About 200,000 black soldiers fought for the North during the Civil War. They were free blacks and escaped slaves. About 35,000 of them were killed in the fighting. Many whites believed that blacks would make poor soldiers. Some argued that blacks should not be allowed to serve. But black troops proved to be brave and valuable. Without black soldiers, the Union might not have won the war.

Harriet was a soldier, too. On the night of June 2, 1863, she helped lead about three hundred black Union soldiers up the Combahee River, near the coast of South Carolina. Harriet and the other soldiers removed bombs the Southerners had planted in the water. Then they sailed on huge gunboats upriver, near some plantations. The soldiers set fire to the plantations, sending the masters and overseers fleeing into the woods.

At first, the slaves on the burning plantations were frightened, but then they ran to the boats. Children screamed and hung on to their mothers' skirts. Harriet carried two pigs for a woman who was toting a child. As she ran, Harriet fell and tore her dress. But she kept hold of the pigs. When it was all over, about 750 slaves had been rescued. "Moses" was saving her people once again.

By the end of the war, many Southern cities—like Charleston, South Carolina—lay in ruins.

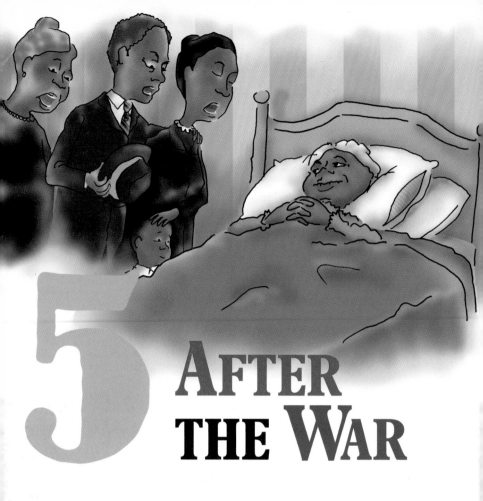

5 AFTER THE WAR

After four years of fighting, the North won the Civil War in April of 1865. And once and for all, slavery was against the law in every state. There would be no more need for the Underground Railroad. Harriet would never have to risk her life to free slaves again.

Harriet wanted to go back to her home in Auburn, New York, to be with her parents. As she boarded the train to go home, the conductor looked at her ticket. It was a half-price ticket. Anyone who fought in the war could ride for half the price. But the conductor told Harriet the train did not carry black people for half price.

This illustration from a newspaper shows members of the House of Representatives celebrating after the Thirteenth Amendment was passed. This law made slavery illegal in every state.

Harriet refused to get off the train, and the man grabbed her arm. He quickly discovered that Harriet was stronger than he was, so he called three other men to help. The four men twisted her arm and shoved her into a baggage car.

Harriet rode in the baggage car all the way home. She was uncomfortable, and her arm was badly hurt. But something else hurt even worse. Slavery was now against the law, but black people were still a long way from being treated equally.

This photo of Harriet was taken during the 1860s.

Some black Americans, like these laborers, found paying jobs after the war. But many had a hard time finding work and feeding their families.

At last, Harriet arrived at home. She enjoyed catching up with her parents and friends. She could rest knowing that no one had to worry about being caught and sent back into slavery.

Harriet was still famous, and she received many visitors. Most were former slaves who were poor and sick. They asked for food, clothes, and medicine. Harriet had almost no money, but she did what she could to help.

Harriet was friends with Susan B. Anthony, an important leader in the fight for women's rights.

The government had refused to pay Harriet for her work during the war. So Harriet worked at whatever jobs she could find. She also raised chickens and grew a vegetable garden. Door to door, Harriet sold the chickens and vegetables. She also earned money by giving speeches. She spoke about fair treatment for black people and women.

In this way, Harriet managed to support herself and her parents, and to help anyone who came to her door. She even opened two schools so children of former slaves could learn to read and write.

In 1869, Harriet married a former slave named Nelson Davis. She had met Nelson at an army base in South Carolina.

PLANTING APPLES

When Harriet was a young slave, her master did not let her eat any apples from the trees he forced her to plant. The little girl decided that when she got older, she would grow apples—not for herself, but for *other* people to eat. Many years later, when Harriet was an old woman, she remembered her plan. Though she hadn't planted apple trees, she said she had still carried out her plan. All the things she had done for other people, like helping slaves to freedom and caring for the needy, were like planting apples for other people to eat.

Nelson died in 1888. Because he had been in the army, Harriet finally received some money from the government. She saved the $20 a month the government gave her. After eight years, she had enough money to buy the land across the street from her house. She opened a home for sick and needy African Americans. In 1911, when Harriet was about ninety-one years old, she moved in there herself.

Harriet was happy in the home. She had many visitors, and she loved to tell stories—especially about the Underground Railroad. On the evening of March 10, 1913, Harriet gathered several friends at her bed. She had pneumonia, and she knew she was going to die soon.

Although Harriet was sick, she was not too weak to sing. She asked her friends to sing with her. As Harriet Tubman lay dying, their voices filled her room.

The Harriet Tubman Home in Auburn, New York

TIMELINE

In the year . . .

1826 Harriet was put to work checking muskrat traps. | Age 6

1830 she was working as hard as a man in the fields.

1835 she was hit in the head with an iron weight after refusing to stop a runaway slave. | Age 15

1844 she married John Tubman.

1849 she escaped from slavery.

1850 she went back into the South to rescue her sister and her sister's family. | Age 30
the Fugitive Slave Law was passed.

1857 she rescued her parents.

1860 she saved a captured slave from a courthouse in Troy, New York.

1861 the Civil War began on April 12.

1862 she traveled to South Carolina to help newly freed slaves.

1863 she led 300 troops up the Combahee River and freed about 750 slaves. | Age 43

1865 the Civil War ended.
she was attacked and thrown in a baggage car by a train conductor and three other men.

1869 she married Nelson Davis.

1888 Nelson Davis died.

1896 she bought the twenty-five acres of land across the road from her house to build a home for the sick and needy. | Age 76

1913 she died of pneumonia on March 10. | Age 93

REMEMBERING HARRIET TUBMAN

Many people honored Harriet for her bravery when she was alive. Queen Victoria of England awarded her a silver medal and invited her to England to celebrate the queen's birthday. Even more honors came to Harriet after she died. A ship was named after her. A park in Auburn, New York, was built in her honor. And in 1995, the United States issued a postage stamp showing Harriet leading slaves to freedom. In Auburn, New York, the Harriet Tubman Home is a museum. It stands as a tribute to her life and her work.

Further Reading

NONFICTION

Bial, Raymond. *The Underground Railroad.* **Boston: Houghton Mifflin Company, 1995.** Gives a history of the Underground Railroad and includes many photos.

Ferris, Jeri. *Go Free or Die: A Story about Harriet Tubman.* **Minneapolis, MN: Carolrhoda Books, Inc., 1993.** Tells the dramatic story of Harriet's escape from slavery. Includes illustrations.

Sullivan, George. *Harriet Tubman.* **New York: Scholastic, 2001.** Tells the story of Harriet Tubman's life, using interviews with Harriet as well as the words of her friends.

Weidt, Maryann N. *Voice of Freedom: A Story about Frederick Douglass.* **Minneapolis, MN: Carolrhoda Books, Inc., 2001.** Tells the story of Frederick Douglass, who was born a slave but escaped at age twenty and worked tirelessly for the antislavery cause. Douglass and Harriet Tubman were good friends.

FICTION

Petry, Ann. *Harriet Tubman: Conductor on the Underground Railroad.* **New York: Harper Trophy, 1996.** The classic, novel-length, fictionalized story of Harriet's life.

Rappaport, Doreen. *Freedom River.* **New York: Jump at the Sun, 2000.** A picture book for older readers. Tells the story of John Parker, an ex-slave who becomes a successful businessman and an active conductor on the Underground Railroad.

WEBSITES

Aboard the Underground Railroad
<http://www.cr.nps.gov/nr/travel/underground/>
Supported by the National Park Service, this website
provides descriptions and photographs of fifty-five historic
places that were associated with the Underground Railroad.
It also includes a history of slavery and a map of the most
common escape routes taken on the Underground Railroad.

The Harriet Tubman Home
<http://www.nyhistory.com/harriettubman/index.htm>
The website for the Harriet Tubman Home, where Harriet
died, which still stands in Auburn, New York. The website
gives Harriet's story, a history of the home, photos, and tour
information.

SELECT BIBLIOGRAPHY

Bradford, Sarah. *Harriet Tubman: The Moses of Her People.*
1886. Reprint, Bedford, MA: Applewood Books, 1993.

Bradford, Sarah. *Scenes in the Life of Harriet Tubman.*
1869. Reprint, Salem, NH: Ayer Company, Publishers,
Inc., 1992.

Conrad, Earl. *Harriet Tubman.* New York: International
Publishers, 1942.

Conrad, Earl. *Harriet Tubman.* Washington, D.C.: The
Associated Publishers, Inc., 1943.

Gorrel, Gena K. *North Star to Freedom: The Story of the
Underground Railroad.* New York: Delacorte Press, 1996.

INDEX

Acknowledgements

For photographs: © Schomburg Center for Research in Black Culture, pp. 4, 42; Georgia Historical Society, p. 7; © North Wind Picture Archives, pp. 8, 14, 16, 18, 19, 20; National Archives, pp. 9, 33, 39; Courtesy of the North Carolina Division of Archives and History, p. 10; Library of Congress, pp. 15, 21, 30, 31, 35, 37, 38; Ohio Historical Society, p. 17; © Sophia Smith Collection/Smith College, p. 24; *Dictionary of American Portraits*, pp. 26, 40; Delaware Public Archives, p. 27; © Leib Image Archives, p. 32; © Lee Snider/CORBIS, p. 43; © U.S. Postal Service, p. 45. Front cover: Library of Congress (photo); Corbis Royalty Free Images (frame). Back cover: © Jim Simondet/Independent Picture Service.

For quoted material: p. 22, Conrad, Earl. *Harriet Tubman.* New York: International Publishers, 1942.

The heart of
King Robert
the Bruce
lies buried
beneath
this marker
at Melrose
Abbey in the
Borders

Loch Katrine from the summit
of Ben Venue, Trossachs

Helmsdale Harbour,
East Sutherland

Traigh Allt Chailgeag, North Sutherland

Kyle of Durness looking south to Foinaven, Sutherland

Neidpath Castle by the River Tweed, Peebles

The Kyle of
Tongue and
Ben Hope from
Island Roan

Poca Buidhe
Flowerdale Forrest
Wester Ross

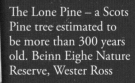

The Lone Pine – a Scots
Pine tree estimated to
be more than 300 years
old. Beinn Eighe Nature
Reserve, Wester Ross

Dunkeld Cathedral,
Perthshire

Scottish Youth Hostel
croft cottage, Howmore,
Isle of South Uist,
Western Isles

Sandwood Bay, North West Sutherland

Skerray Township, Sutherland

Torrisdale Bay and mouths of the rivers Borgie and Naver, Sutherland

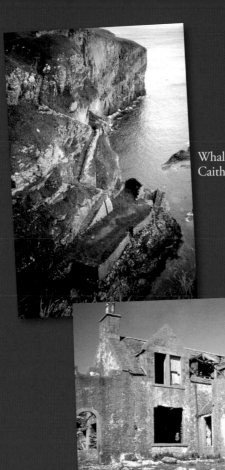

Whaligoe Steps,
Caithness

Windhouse: the haunted
house on the Island of Yell,
Shetland

Eilean Donan
Castle, Loch
Duich along the
Road to the Isles

Coldbackie Beach looking towards Island Roan in North Sutherland

Castle Varrich and Ben Hope, Tongue, Sutherland

Stromness, Orkney Islands

Urquhart
Castle,
Loch Ness,
Inverness-shire

Hugh Miller's fossil beds, The Black Isle

Crichton Castle, Midlothian

People make songs about your big cousin,
Extravagantly sprawled over mountain after mountain.
They tear him up and he goes off to England
On the bumpers of cars, on shiny radiators.
But you are more beautiful and you blossom first,
In square feet and raggedy circles.
Your blue travels a hundred yards
That are the main road for bees.
If I were an adder, I'd choose you
For my royal palace. My sliding tongue
Would savour the thin scent
Of your boudoirs and banqueting halls.
A modest immodesty is a good thing,
Little blaze of blue on a rock face.
I'll try it myself. Will the bees come,
The wild bees with their white noses?

Edinburgh, "The City of Literature", is as vibrant and vital today as it was in the time of Scott and Burns. Find its magic, as the poet William Ernest Henley did when he visited the "Athens of the North":

A late lark twitters from the quiet skies;
And from the west,
There the sun, his day's work ended,
Lingers as in content,
There falls on the old, gray city
An influence luminous and serene,
A shining peace.

23.
The Story of Windhouse on the Island of Yell, Shetland

I believe in ghosties and ghoulies and things that go bump in the night; in hobgoblins, water sprites, witches and warlocks and the whole bang-shoot of the unexplored, mysterious nether regions of this mortal coil. This is why the ruins of Windhouse on the Island of Yell in Shetland made me uneasy.

Tattered walls, once pitch-pine and lath-and-plaster clad, seep dampness. Broken roof beams spear-point the gloom. Empty window frames gape like missing teeth. The staircase hung crookedly. Most of its steps are missing. My spine tingled. I turned to speak to my wife, Ann, to ask her if she felt uncomfortable. She was nowhere to be seen. Then I heard her call from outside, "Come on, Bruce, let's get on with our walk."

This was my introduction to Windhouse and I had no idea then that the house was haunted by not one, but by a whole family of spirits; the Lady in Silk, the ghost of a woman whose skeleton, with a broken neck, was found under floorboards at the foot of the staircase; the Man in Black, a tall spectre in a black cloak most frequently seen outside the kitchen window; the ghost of a child whose remains were discovered built into the kitchen wall; and, to keep them company, the ghost of a black dog.

In 1995, the Shetland writer and author Johnathan Wills spoke to Greta Manson, whose mother, Ruby, had worked as a maid at Windhouse in the 1920s when the estate was owned by Mr James Gordon. She remembered being there. "I was once in the house as a child and I was not very happy about it. There was what they call 'The Lady in Silk' who shuffles round you three times before disappearing."

Greta recalled, "One night my mother was sitting in the kitchen when she heard a child wailing. She thought it was the other maids trying to frighten her but then she heard it again, closer. When it cried a third time and she felt the touch of a little hand on her cheek, she ran out. Later they found the remains of a baby, walled up next to where she'd been sitting."

I know about these things. I have spoken to a ghost. In 1968, we bought an old farmhouse, Hardriding, near the Roman Wall in Northumberland. Mrs Smith, the previous owner, died peacefully one evening after supper in the Morning Room. In the middle of the night, I think it was May, I got up and went downstairs. I don't know why.

A woman swept past me and I followed her into the drawing room. It seemed to be the natural thing to do. "Now," she said, sitting down in a chair before the fire, "tell me about yourself and your family." We talked. She was kind. She said she was glad that we lived in her house.

I discovered later that it was the first anniversary of Mrs Smith's death and I described her perfectly to neighbours who had known her for years. But I was never uncomfortable with that experience. We lived at Hardriding for a long time with our wonderful, supportive friend. How would I have reacted to being confronted with the most widely reported ghostly appearances at Windhouse? I don't know. Andrew Mathewson, the schoolmaster at East Yell, wrote about it in 1863:

"It so happened that a vessel of much importance got embayed on the north west of Shetland on a Christmas evening [in the early 1800s] and was wrecked at the Dall of Lumbister. The Master escaped safe to land with nothing but his sheaf knife strapped firm and his poleaxe in his hand.

"On his recovery from being almost drowned, he wandered inland in search of relief, which brought him in full view of Windhouse. Hither he hastened forward as the day was drawing to its close and on reaching the mansion he was welcomed as a friend and refreshed as a brother."

The account then relates how the seaman was surprised to find everyone at Windhouse busy packing and preparing for departure. He asked his host, Mr Neven, where they were going.

"To this request he received for answer that for this night of the year, namely Yule E'en or the 24th of every December, that he would have to seek lodgings for himself, as no mortal who had ever attempted to sleep in the house that night was ever found alive in the morning but was destroyed and slain by some evil spirit from the sea called Trows," the Shetland name for goblins.

The ship's captain persuaded Mr Neven to let him remain at Windhouse so that he could confront the demon. Our hero fortified himself in the library, where he drank a lot of Neven's wine, and ate a lot of the food his considerate host had prepared for his coming ordeal. The captain slept a little. Drank more wine, read a book and composed himself.

"At one o'clock a sound arose as of rolling thunder and the whole fabric of the house shook and trembled as if going to ruins . . . to sit still and die so ignominiously was not his desire. In the name and strength of the Blessed he made ready, felt his dagger and grasped his axe, tore down the barricades from the door and threw back the bar."

A dark shape fled from him and he pursued it towards Mid Yell Voe. Just before the creature reached the sea, the Captain hurled his axe, striking it in the head. When he examined the body, all that he could make out was a "shapeless mass". He disposed of the creature in a large hole, covered it with earth and then formed the fence around it, which still remains.

The Windhouse ghosts are a mystery. Why do they persistently haunt the dwelling? The deeds of a previous owner, Ninian Neven, might provide a clue. Ninian was a notary public, a latter-day lawyer and a rogue. When John Swanieson, the master of Windhouse in 1614, died, Ninian was asked to attend to the transfer of the estate to John's son and heir, James.

Ninian contrived, through duplicity and manipulation of the law, to oust Swanieson and acquire the estate for himself. James was no match for the glib-tongued lawyer and eight years after the death of John, Ninian was master of Windhouse. In succeeding years, he bought land throughout Yell and soon became the island's most important and feared landowner. Perhaps the Windhouse ghosts are the souls of those he persecuted.

Ruby Manson claimed that an old woman put a curse on the Neven family when they evicted people to make way for sheep: "She told the laird that neither he nor his progeny would ever prosper and that one day sheep would wander through his house, as indeed they do today." When Ann and I were there we found evidence of sheep aplenty.

The Neven family was eventually forced to sell the estate in 1884 when John Harrison, an up-and-coming Lerwick fish merchant, bought it. John had grandiose ideas about his status in the community and it was he who added the crenellated abutments and entrance porch to Windhouse. Nevertheless, he was no more fortunate in his property than the Nevens had been and was declared bankrupt within ten years.

The next owner, William Gordon, was a soldier and when he died in 1919 in the Middle East, his nephew, James, inherited Windhouse and lived there into the 1930s. James was the last person to occupy the famously haunted dwelling and it was during that time that the estate farm was let to an eminent local family, the Johnsons. But the eminently sensible Johnsons chose to settle at Setter, a step south from dreaded Windhouse.

Windhouse began to die. The body deteriorated and the garden became a wilderness. Winter storms ravaged the once-bold abutments and surrounding walls. They crumbled and collapsed. Only the stark uprights of the entrance pillars are left to guard the way in. Above the front door is the Neven family coat of arms, a fading affair of shields and plumes surmounted by barely discernable words carved in stone: "Faithful," and, perhaps, "doing good to all"?

I turned from the somber ruin and joined Ann on the hill. Together, we tramped the golden moor to the deserted village of Vollister on the east shore of Whale Firth, near to where the slayer of the Windhouse trow was wrecked. But unlike Windhouse, the tumbled ruins here greeted us happily and, borne about the soft wind, I heard the sound of dogs barking and children's laughter echoing amidst the grey stones.

24.
Dornie to Durness

Laughter from the bar of the Dornie Hotel mingled with curlew call from the shores of Loch Duich. I looked towards Eilean Donan Castle, the ancient home of Clan Macrae. The clan paid a heavy price for joining the 1719 uprising in support of the Old Pretender, son of the deposed King James II. In order to dislodge a contingent of Spanish soldiers sheltering there, the castle was reduced to rubble by the British frigate, *HMS Worcester*.

I was at the start point of a fantastic journey, from Dornie in Inverness-shire, through the North West Highlands to Durness in Sutherland. I nodded goodbye to Eilean Donan, wondering if Clan Macrae and Spanish ghosts still haunted its elegantly refurbished halls. Half an hour later, humour restored, I was in Plockton, on the shores of Loch Carron. A boisterous Labrador dashed in and out of the shallow waters of the bay. Visitors luxuriated in warm sunlight.

But most residents were preparing for church. I remembered another Sunday morning, many years ago, when, as children, we spent a holiday there. My father was an angler and, thinking that with everyone in church it would be safe, he decided to go fishing. Sunday fishing was much frowned upon then. When church came out, my father hid from sight by lying in the bottom of the boat. How an empty boat came to be there, or how it managed to moor itself again, remained a mystery.

Plockton is an artists' paradise. Miriam Drysdale runs painting holidays from her home in an old manse overlooking the loch: "I managed to rent the Plockton Small Boat Sailing Clubhouse as studios, just beside the little jetty. It's great! Warm, big sink and good light and ideal for all painter-persons," she said. As well as artists, you may also meet cattle tramping the main street, for this is still a working crofting community.

A wondrous road winds along the shore of Loch Carron, passing a tiny, lighthouse-pricked island. The view north into the Applecross Forest is unforgettable: Beinn Bhan (896m) and the peaks of Sgurr a'Chaorachain (792m) and Meall Gorm (949m) enfolding the tortuous track over Bealach na Ba (626m), "The Pass of the Cattle". Within six miles from Tornapress at the mouth of the River Kishorn, the road rises to over 610 metres. The view from the top is magnificent: westwards to the Cuillin on Skye and, in the distance, a glimpse of the "Heather Isles" of the Outer Hebrides.

Back on the main road, descending into Torridon, I admired three of Scotland's best-loved mountains: Beinn Alligin (The Jeweled Hill), Liathach (The Grey One) and Beinn Eighe (The Big Red Peak). Beyond these is a Scottish gem, Poca Bhuidhe (the yellow stone), a bothy at the head of Loch na h-Oidhche (The Loch of the Night). Ann and I hiked the four miles out to the bothy a few years ago and spent happy days enjoying the "large religion of the hills".

Many West Highland mountains are composed of red Torridonian sandstone and are often surrounded, in their lower levels, by evidence of retreating ice flows, 10,000 years ago; small, rounded hillocks show where heavier rocks and other debris dropped through the ice sheet, forming distinctive features known as "hummocky moraines".

North from Gairloch (The Long Loch), I paid my respects to Osgood Mackenzie's famous Inverewe Garden where 2,500 different species of trees and plants cover fifty acres. It was raining but this did not stop visitors from enjoying themselves. Osgood was famous for his prowess with gun and fishing rod, described in his book *A Hundred Years of Sport in the Highlands*, and has the dubious reputation of shooting the last osprey in Wester Ross.

From Inverewe, before the tiny township of Laide, is a hill with a view. The panorama from the roadside at Cnoc nan Colunnan is stunning. To the south, the majesty of the peaks and ridges you have driven round is laid out in a panorama of sheer delight. The road ahead margins Little Loch Broom.

Beyond Dundonnell, stop and look back to An Teallach (1,062m), "The Forge". Tradition has it that the mountain is named thus because the sunset glow from An Teallach's red sandstone corries resembled embers in a blacksmith's forge.

This road, from Dundonnell to Braemore Junction, is known as "Destitution Road". It was built in the aftermath of the 1851 potato famine, when Highland people starved. But the authorities considered that giving the populace food would encourage them in idleness. Therefore, to alleviate hardship, whilst Lowland granaries bulged with corn, the local lairds, ministers and the powers that be decided that the people should work for their relief. The "Destitution Road" is their memorial.

Ullapool is bright and bustling. A dozen different languages may be heard as you walk the harbour front. Fishing boats bob by the pier and hotels and restaurants have an almost Mediterranean feel. Visitors linger over al fresco meals whilst the inevitable cat begs for scraps. The town is "new" in Highland terms, built by the British Fisheries Association in 1788 to exploit the herring fishing industry. Ullapool is still a busy fishing port today and one of the main ferry terminals for a magical journey over the broken waters of the Minch to the Western Isles.

It is also a jumping-off point for the Summer Isles, where I next stopped to examine a more modern construction, the temperature-controlled domain of the Hydroponicum at Achiltibuie. Hydroponics is the art of growing plants without soil. Water does the work of transporting all of the plant's nutrient requirements to the roots. Mark Irvine, former owner of the Summer Isles Hotel, set up the Hydroponicum to ensure a regular supply of fresh vegetables for his internationally renowned restaurant. I relaxed in semi-tropical warmth with a cup of coffee and a Highland banana.

A narrow road leads north round the coast from Achiltibuie into Assynt, "the broken lands". To the east, the mountains of the Inverpolly National Nature Reserve dominate the horizon: Stac Pollaidh (612m), Cul Mor (849m), Cul Beag (769m), and the dramatic thrust of Suilven (731m), the peak the Vikings called their pillar mountain, "Sul-val". Entering Assynt is like coming home for Ann and me. We have spent some of our happiest moments here, hill-walking, fishing, watching birds, discovering wildflowers, bickering over map references, being together.

We also bought a lot of books at Achins Bookshop, the most remote bookshop in Europe. Achins is just in Sutherland. The boundary between Ross-shire and Sutherland is the centre-line of the River Kirkaig and Achins is hidden amidst the trees above this rocky stream. When I called, in the absence of her mum and dad, young Kathleen Dickson was holding fort. It had been a busy day but she greeted me with a captivating Highland smile.

After driving through Assynt to Kylesku, I swept importantly across the graceful bridge over Loch a'Chairn Bhain and on to Scourie, the land of Clan Mackay. Ann and I first visited Scourie in, well, a lot of years ago. We stayed at the Scourie Hotel and spent our time trout fishing. Our principal objective was a tiny, unnamed lochan in the hills to the south of Ben Stack. It contained a wise old trout known as "Granddad", desired by every angler who knew the location of his home. Granddad eluded all our efforts and, indeed, everyone else's.

To the best of my knowledge, Granddad died of old age.

Beyond Scourie, by Tarbet, you will find "the restaurant at the edge of the world", specialising in fantastic seafood. Big it is not. It is an extension to the front of a traditional croft cottage, built by Julian Pearce when he was a youth of sixteen years. The restaurant is not licensed but what it does provide is miraculous cooking – prawns, crab and lobster that are often served within hours of being caught. Arm yourself with a bottle of Chablis before setting out.

Julian's wife, Jackie, who does the cooking, believes seafood should be served unadorned. Jackie's daughters, Rebecca and Lucy, do the work behind the scenes. I asked Jackie what her most memorable moment had been.

She pondered. "After a guest finished eating, he asked me to marry him."

"Julian?" I inquired.

"No, not Julian," Jackie said, "the guest. He had really enjoyed his meal!"

As I approached journey's end, driving over the watershed north of

Rhiconich in the shadow of Foinaven (914m), the underlying rock structure changed again. Here, a limestone outcrop surfaces and blesses the landscape with an amazing array of wildflowers. Across the sands of the Kyle of Durness, Grudie Cottage glistened. Also glistening, but for entirely different reasons, were the group of people I found waiting to cross to Cape Wrath. The ferryman was there but the bus driver was not. A few "Highland minutes" later, he arrived.

Close to the Cape Wrath Hotel, an imposing whitewashed building that guards the narrows of the Kyle and is now a private dwelling, I discovered one of Scotland's most important sheepdog trials. Jock Sutherland from Sangomore, who travels to trials throughout the UK, told me that some of Britain's top dog-handlers were taking part. His bright-eyed, tongue-lolling, happy sheepdogs, Maid and Nell, eager for action, nodded in agreement.

At the end of my journey, I said hello to another important person, John Lennon of The Beatles fame. As a youth, John often visited relatives at Durness and a memorial garden at the newly built village hall commemorates this connection. I looked out over Sango Bay. How long had it been since I set off? A curlew poked and probed along the margins of the tide and I remembered the sound of curlew at Eilean Donan. A haunting call, "as desolate, as beautiful as your loved places, mountainy marshes and glistening mud-flats by the stealthy sea."

25.
Highland Museum, Kingussie and Newtonmore

I looked at the ink-spattered paper on my desk and shuffled uncomfortably. It wasn't my fault. The steel nib of the wooden-shafted pen seemed to have a life of its own. Pupils behind me giggled at my discomfiture. The thumb and forefinger of my right hand were stained black. There was a spot of ink on my shirt. Mrs Brownlee loomed over me. "Please, Miss, I didn't mean to do it, honest," I pleaded.

"That's just not good enough, Bruce," she said. "You must try harder, otherwise you will have to pay the penalty." Mrs Brownlee glared crossly and flexed the thick leather strap she was holding.

Thankfully, it was all "pretend". I was not a child again, only an adult visitor to the splendid Newtonmore Highland Folk Museum (HFM) schoolroom a few miles south from Inverness. But it had been a close-run thing because the reality of the experience had brought childhood memories flooding back. The classroom was an exact replica of the one where I had struggled in vain so many years ago with pen and ink at same unforgiving wooden desk. With the familiar hollow for holding the pencils I never remembered to bring to school and the same intimidating white ceramic inkwell.

Anna Brownlee is in fact a wonderful communicator, humorous and kindly, and with the sort of personality that brightens the dullest of days. The classroom once housed destitute Glasgow children whose fathers had been killed during the First World War. Its original location was near Kirkhill, north of Inverness, where it was intended to be temporary. The school closed in 1987 and HFM acquired the property, dismantled it and reconstructed it at Newtonmore. The walls are covered with 1930s maps. There is a "nature table", blackboard, writing slates, games cupboard, children's paintings on the walls, coat-hanging pegs and, dominating all, the teacher's majestic desk.

The HFM Newtonmore site covers an area of eighty acres and is one and a half kilometres in length. Everything about this vibrant open-air museum inspires. The care, attention to detail and the meticulous planning and veracity of the exhibits demonstrates the highest standards of excellence. Clearly, this is a labour of love for those involved, from Ross Noble, the curator, and his staff, to each of his forty-strong, part-time team of helpers. Their most notable characteristics are unwavering courtesy and patience, fortified with a thorough knowledge of the exhibits they attend. From start to finish, everyone I met was welcoming.

The original museum, Am Fasgadh, "The Shelter", was established in 1944 in Kingussie and was the inspirational dream of a remarkable woman, Dr Isabel Frances Grant (1887–1983). Dr Grant visited Scandinavia during the 1920s and was impressed by the importance placed there upon folk museums – museums that captured the culture of the people and how they lived and worked and played. Dr Grant was determined to replicate that philosophy in the Highlands of Scotland, initially by opening a museum on Iona in 1936 and then, when the collection outgrew the space available, by moving to Kingussie.

In a time when government subsidies and grants for small museums were unheard of, Dr Grant used her own money to further the development of her invention. When she retired in 1954, she arranged for the museum to be taken into the care of a trust controlled by Scotland's primary universities: St Andrews, Edinburgh, Glasgow and Aberdeen. But as the museum continued to expand, they too found it hard to appropriately finance Am Fasgadh. Consequently, in 1975 and largely due to the support of Councillor Sandy Russell of Newtonmore, the leisure and recreation committee of the Highland Regional Council agreed to take over responsibility for the museum.

There are tens of thousands of items and artefacts in the collection and, due to limitations of space, only a small part of them can de displayed at any one time. What is on show, however, is utterly absorbing. I spent one day at the Kingussie site and the following day at Newtonmore. In order to do so, I had to stay overnight in Kingussie and chose the Columba House Hotel as my base. This was a happy choice, not only because it is one of the most comfortable and friendly places in which I have ever stayed, but also because I heard about the mystery of "the lost priory".

Myra Shearer had owned the hotel for sixteen years and as we chatted over pre-dinner drinks, she explained: "I was working in the garden one afternoon when, suddenly, the earth simply fell away to expose a flight of stairs. I followed them down and found myself in an underground room measuring approximately ten feet by eight feet. There were bits of dishes and plates lying about, but what really fascinated me was a stone lintel, at floor level, which suggested that there might be more rooms at a lower level." Could Myra have stumbled on the thirteenth-century priory that tradition says was located in the vicinity?

I walked from the hotel to the HFM Kingussie site and fell in with a bearded crofter crouching over a peat fire on the floor of a Black House. Men from the Island of Lewis in the Outer Hebrides had erected the building. I stooped low to enter: "Is it all right to come in?" I called. A kettle was suspended over glowing embers.

"Good morning! Yes, in you come to the fire." Peter Bruce, an HFM part-timer and dressed for the role he played, explained how the Black House was built, why it took the shape and form it did, and how it was used. Peter, a retired art teacher from Shetland, was captivating.

Pitman Lodge, a Georgian town house, hosts the HFM reception area, where young Eilidh Macpherson greeted me with a mile-high smile. Eilidh's mother, Gail, helps out here with demonstrations of spinning and weaving. Her grandmother, Iris Robertson, a splendidly happy woman, also works with the HFM. I could have spent a week at Pitman Lodge. It contains a treasure trove of magnificent objects: snuff boxes, delicate china, musical instruments, kitchen utensils, portable baths with their own internal water-heating systems, costumes, quaichs, wooden plates and bowls. There is a farming museum, complete with stables, harness pack saddles, ploughs, harrows and threshing machines, and a dairy with butter churns and cheese presses.

Adjacent to Pitman Lodge is the MacRobert House with its textile crafts room, where you can find out about wool spinning – from using a simple spindle, then the "muckle wheel", turned by hand, to the seventeenth-century treadle spinning wheel. But for me, the MacRobert House Furniture Gallery was most spectacular. There is something unique about the strong smell of well-polished wood and the collection on display here is illustrious. There is an amazing two-tier box-bed, built in 1702, part of a double unit that probably had two lower and two upper beds providing sleeping quarters for a whole family. I tiptoed past. Who might still be asleep there?

Down at the Newtonmore HFM site, I caught a courtesy bus to visit Baile Gean. Geoff Pittard, the driver, proudly showed off his vehicle, a masterpiece sit-up-and-beg replica of 1930s public transport. The green leather-clad seats were supremely comfortable. Baile Gean means "The Township of Goodwill" and arriving there is like stepping back into another age. It is a recreation of an early-eighteenth-century Highland community, complete with houses, barns, corn kiln and shieling huts, based upon current archaeological research. The township is surrounded by mature trees, loud with birdcall and enchanting glimpses of native red squirrels amidst the old branches.

I expected at any moment to see residents going about their daily tasks. And I did. HFM helpers, in period costumes, invited me into their lives. Wendy Smith was busy woodturning but stopped to introduce me to her friend, Gerry Smith. We wandered down to the duck pond to inspect a newly arrived red-brown pig. Clutching a bundle of thatch, Gerry chatted with Wendy whilst she fed the ducks. Before I left, I peeked into Wendy's "home". She was sitting before a cooking pot. A beam of light slanted down from the roof to give her an almost ethereal presence, a "solitary Highland lass".

The animals at Netwonmore are in the care of Eric Stewart, previously a farmer from the Glens of Angus, now working for HFM. He has a fine flock of Blackface sheep that were busy cropping grass fields bounded by drystone built walls. The walls themselves are fascinating, demonstrating different dyking techniques from various areas of the Highlands. Bob Powell, HFM Assistant Curator, agricultural historian and registered farmer, introduced me to the latest arrival: Jubilee, a Clydesdale foal snuggled up to his mother, Rosie, and born on 4 June, the date of HM The Queen's Jubilee.

At the farm steading, I caught up with another HFM character, Billy Kirk, whose father had farmed the Newtonmore site before it was acquired by the museum. Billy took me to a small corrugated-iron clad house. He explained: "When visitors came here during the summer months, the family would rent their big house to them, to make some money, and move in here." The little house was simply but comfortably furnished in the 1930s style. Billy lit the fire and put the kettle on for tea.

As I nursed my cup and the dreams my visit had evoked, I thought of these long-gone Highland people – the clamour of the school bell, calling children to their studies; the warm smell of animals lying together in a hay-filled byre; the busy clatter of a butter churn; spluttering fir candles lighting an evening entertainment. I remembered, also, words written by the founder of the HFM, Isabel Grant: "I hope and dare to believe that in this little museum there does exist some sense of the spirit of the people of the Highlands, the race from which I am so proud to have sprung."

The Highland Folk Museum has two complementary venues, Kingussie and Newtonmore, two and a half miles apart. They are located on the A86 and are easily found by following signposts off the A9. There is free parking at both sites. Allow at least two hours for a visit to the Kingussie site and four hours to visit Newtonmore.

For further information, contact: Highland Folk Museum, Kingussie Road, Newtonmore, Scotland PH20 1AY; Tel: 01540 673551; Fax: 01540 673693; Website: www.highlandfolk.com

26.
Nothing to Do and Not Enough Time to Do It

An acquaintance in London once asked me where I lived. "Tongue," I said, "in North Sutherland."

He seemed puzzled. "All year round?" he asked.

I glanced from his skyscraper office window, twenty levels up. The street below was nose-to-tail packed with cars. The pavements were crowded. "Yup," I replied happily, "all year round."

Our cottage overlooks Castle Varrich, a sixteenth-century Clan Mackay fortress guarding the shallow waters of the Kyle of Tongue. Our previous home was near Loch Watten in Caithness. Across the loch, Caithness mountains Scaraben, Smean and graceful Morven lined our horizon.

Our children thrived in the freedom and security of the far north. They explored with us the wilderness of the peat lands of the Flow Country; learned from us the friendly names of its flora and fauna; enjoyed with us the sharp bite of winter storms and the precious calm of long summer evenings.

There was always so much to do. I was the Secretary of the Wick Arts Club for a number of years when we welcomed performers of international repute to play for us – pianists, string quartets, ballet and opera, et al. Caithness also hosts a major summer arts festival, Northlands, celebrating the finest in Highland and Celtic culture.

The longest day, 21 June, is busy with midnight bowls tournaments, trout fishing outings, golf matches and midsummer parties. Visitors from all over the world brighten these gatherings, mingling and making friends with local people. Scotland's two most northerly counties provided for our every need, spiritual and physical. They will do the same for you.

Here are some of my favorite Caithness and Sutherland expeditions. The list is not exhaustive and is, of necessity, limited. But I hope that it will encourage you to join us. Come and explore the solitude of our ragged cliffs and silent beaches. Climb our mountains. Listen to the echo of time amidst sentinel tumbled stones that were alive with the sound of laughter 5,000 years ago.

SLETELL VILLAGE AND SKERRAY TOWNSHIP, SUTHERLAND (Open all year)

The deserted village of Sletell graces green pastures looking across the sea to Island Roan. North Country sheep and handsome cattle graze contentedly. The sense of peace is a tangible presence. When Ann and I last walked there, we lunched in the lee of one of the ruined cottages. By the shores of a cliff-top lochan, an otter played with her cubs.

Begin your adventure at the croft museum in Skerray. A summer exhibition features the life and times of Sletell and you will be given directions to the start of the Sletell track; an easy walk, there and back in three hours including plenty of time to explore the village and enjoy its wonderful setting.

Also explore the Millennium Memorial Forest at Borgie, ten minutes drive from Skerray Post Office. Native trees were planted here in a Celtic circle, their names following the order of the old Gaelic tree alphabet. A path leads to the centre where stones from houses burned during the eighteenth-century Sutherland Clearances are shaped in the form a magical leaf.

WORLD KNOTTY CHAMPIONSHIPS, LYBSTER, CAITHNESS (August)

During the Caithness herring fishings of the nineteenth century, Lybster was an important centre of the industry and Lybster fishermen, to entertain themselves when not fishing for herring, invented "Knotty". Bert Mowat, a proprietor of the Portland Arms Hotel in Lybster, a few miles south from

Wick, is said to have discovered the rules for the game in an old Gaelic Bible.

The game is a cross between shinty and hockey, played using a cork float from a herring net as a ball. Wooden staves from herring barrels were used to hit the ball. Hazel twigs stuck in the ground formed goal posts. When a goal was scored, to keep the score, a knot was tied in a length of fishing line.

Marshall Bowman, a local schoolteacher who acts as referee, explained: "There are seven-a-side teams. Last year, fifteen teams competed, including 'Gunn's Guzzlers', 'Gunettes' and 'Rita's Boys', named after local businesses. Men compete for a cup, ladies' teams compete for a Shield."

George Carter, another Knotty aficionado, told me it was a vigorous day out and that the game was played with a lot of spirit, some of it taken from straw-coloured bottles. "Bruised shins, lumps and knocks are taken as well," he added, "but everyone enjoys themselves."

CAITHNESS COUNTY SHOW AND WICK GALA WEEK
(July and August)

One of my Caithness farmer friends was to be presented to Princess Anne, the Princess Royal, at the County Show. He told me he was not the slightest bit awed by the prospect. In the event, he confessed, when Princess Anne asked him a simple question about farming, he was overwhelmed and speechless. You will be also, by the beauty and quality of the stock on display at the show.

A week after the County Show, the Royal Burgh of Wick bursts into bloom during Gala Week. Every day is interest-packed: decorated floats tour the town; the Gala Queen is crowned; there are children's talent competitions, horse racing and cycle races; Scottish concerts and pipe bands get toes tapping; and there are tennis competitions, vintage car exhibitions, football matches and old-time dancing.

The highlight of the week is the final evening when there is a huge bonfire and firework display on the banks of the Wick River. We always took our family along. I rarely saw much of the fireworks. My younger daughter,

Jean, insisted on being perched upon my shoulders to get a better view. In her excitement, she invariably clasped her hands tightly over my eyes. Fireworks? What fireworks?

DURNESS, SUTHERLAND

Durness, in North West Sutherland, is an essential venue for a family day out. It offers something for everyone. I know, because Clan Sandison has been enjoying the delights of this happy Highland community for more years than I care to remember.

I love game fishing. Durness has four of the most exciting trout lochs in Europe: Caladail, Borralie, Croispol and Lanlish. There is a wonderful little 9-hole golf course, ideal for the pleasure of those so afflicted. My wife, Ann, studies wild flowers. The lime rich soil here hosts an amazing array of plants, including several species of orchid, mountain everlasting and mountain aven.

Balnakeil Beach is an irresistible attraction for children, a wide sweep of golden sand backed by tall dunes. The shallow waters are safe for splashing, whilst older children can surfboard and fall off sailboards to their hearts' content. There are walks from the beach out to Faraid Head, a round trip of six miles, where the cliffs abound with seabirds including, during spring months, firework-beaked puffins.

The great caves at Smoo to the east of Durness also demand inspection. The Scottish novelist Sir Walter Scott, the wizard of the north, is just one of many famous visitors to these spectacular limestone caves. The principal cave is 61m in length, 15m in height, and close by, another cave contains a 24m high waterfall that is a thunderous roar after heavy rain.

For rest and recuperation, call at Balnakeil Craft Village, where craftspersons and artists work and display the results of their talents. Best of all, stop at my favorite bookshop, the Loch Croispol Bookshop, the most northerly bookshop on mainland Scotland. They offer first-class food, a wide range of teas and real coffee, all served with grace and charm. There is a children's section complete with toys to keep curious minds active. Browse the shelves and plan your next adventure.

WICK HARBOUR EVENING, CAITHNESS (July)

The Royal National Lifeboat Institution is entirely supported by voluntary contributions from the public and has been saving lives at sea for 178 years. The Wick Harbour Evening is a fund-raising event organized by the RNLI and it has become a "must" for visitors and locals alike.

Sales stalls are set out, there is music and line dancing, and activities to keep everyone happy and busy. The airport and Highland Council fire engines and an ambulance are available for supervised inspection by children of all ages, but the highlight of the event is a harbour raft race.

Teams, including the police force, fire brigade and the RNLI, compete in this less than serious maritime escapade. The result is always unpredictable and always incident-packed. In 2003, much to the hilarity of the assembled crowd, the RNLI raft sank having covered no more than six metres of the course, requiring the crew to be ignominiously "rescued" by their colleagues.

SANDWOOD BAY, SUTHERLAND

Ann and I sat on black basalt rocks that centre Sandwood Bay in North West Sutherland. A figure splashing in the surf caught our eye. Could this be the famous Sandwood mermaid? I grabbed my camera. In the eighteenth century, a local shepherd, Sandy Gunn, reported seeing a mermaid at Sandwood sitting on a rock gazing wistfully out to sea. Three learned lawyers from Edinburgh, and lawyers don't come much more "learned" than those from Auld Reekie, could not fault his story.

As we watched, a grey seal, rather than a mermaid, emerged from the waves and laboriously hauled itself onto the deserted yellow sands. Not as spectacular as a mermaid, perhaps, but just as magical and enthralling. We relaxed, refilled our coffee cups and watched the graceful creature as we finished our picnic lunch.

Sandwood is one of the loveliest bays in the world, home for 3,000-mile-old azure and white Atlantic waves. Dark cliffs march northwards to Cape Wrath, the Vikings' "turning point" on their annual journey from Denmark to visit their Scottish domains. The gaunt stack of Am Buachaille, "The Herdsman", guards the southern entrance to the bay. Sandwood Loch sparkles in summer sunlight behind steep dunes.

The track to Sandwood Bay starts a few miles to the west of Oldshoremore where there is room to park your car. There and back is a comfortable eight miles along a good track. Nevertheless, wear stout walking boots and carry Ordnance Survey Sheet 9, Cape Wrath, Second Series, Scale 1:50,000. Just how long your journey takes depends entirely on how long you choose to stand or sit and stare. But be warned. It is so captivating that you could be there forever.

HIGHLAND GAMES (July onwards)

Charlie Simpson from Wick was one of the leading "heavies" in the north Highland Games circuit. He is still a formidable presence. Less well-known is his remarkable memory, particularly when it comes to reciting the poetry of Robert Burns. Charlie is always in demand for Burns Supper engagements. I asked him to give me the dates for the Caithness and Sutherland games and he reeled them off faster than I could write them down.

During the summer season, no matter where you are, you will generally find a Highland Games event "just around the corner": the Assynt Games at Lochinver, Halkirk Games, and the principal Caithness event at John O'Groats; games at Dunrobin Castle, Dornoch, Durness, Dunbeath and Helmsdale. Watching the games is almost as exhausting as taking part. The sheer energy and enthusiasm engendered is a living, vibrant presence. Whichever venue you choose, believe me, you and all your "clan" will have a memorable day out.

Now, you will have to excuse me, things to do. Meg Telfer, a local artist, has a pottery class starting at Skerray this evening. And I have to sort out my fishing tackle for a sea-trout fishing expedition on Loch Hope. Then there is a sailing regatta on Loch Shin at Lairg. Iain Sutherland from the Wick Heritage Society is screening, for one night only, archive films from days of the Caithness herring fishings. Will I be able to fit in the céilidh on Saturday night? Perhaps I should ask my London acquaintance for advice?

27.
Highland Railway

James Hamish Mackay stood on the railway platform at Kinbrace in Sutherland. It was winter 1955, one of the fiercest anyone could remember. Huge snowdrifts blocked the line north. As he watched, five hissing steam engines were linked together, ready to "charge" the drifts in an attempt to clear the blockage.

Hamish was ten years old and he should have been in school, but the sound and smell of impending battle transfixed him. The engines reversed slowly south, out of sight. A few minutes later they reappeared, gathering speed, red coal fragments spitting from their funnels, sparks flying from their wheels.

The noise was tremendous. The ground shook. As the convoy raced through the tiny hamlet, house windows shattered. But the line was cleared. From that moment, Hamish knew exactly what he wanted to be when he left school. When he did, he worked on north railway lines for twenty years, reaching the rank of Inspector.

Hamish now runs the famous Craggan Hotel in Melness, overlooking the Kyle of Tongue in North Sutherland. But he has never forgotten these days, which were amongst the happiest of his life. When I talked to him recently, I asked how he got his first job. "I was told to stand on Kinbrace Station and wait for the Inverness train. The chief would meet me there and interview me.

"The train just went straight through. I didn't know what to do, so I went to the office to ask what had happened. The telephone was ringing when I went in and the call was for me. 'Hamish, this is the chief. You are big enough, you'll do!' The chief had been on the footplate of the engine and had seen me standing on the platform and was phoning from Forsinard, the next station up the line."

If you love railways and viewing wide-open spaces in relative comfort, buy a ticket for one of the last and least-known great railway journeys of the world, from Inverness to Wick/Thurso in Caithness. Along the way, surrounded by outstanding scenery, you will be presented with a succession of memorable cameos of Scottish history.

Wick and Thurso are the most northerly railway stations on mainland Britain, eighty miles north from Inverness as the crow flies. By car the journey takes two hours, by bus just under three. But by train the travelling time is four hours.

The railway covers a distance of 160 miles; wandering round indented sea-blue firths, following fertile straths and peat-stained rivers, stopping at small Highland towns and villages en route before striking north east across the magnificent wilderness of the Flow Country.

When winter storms batter our northern senses and blizzards block the steep cliff-top road, the railway line is often the only way either into or out of Caithness. Although passengers may shiver a bit during winter journeys, at least they know that they will get there, eventually.

Work on the line began in Inverness on 19 September 1860 when Lady Matheson, wife of Sir Alexander Matheson, the principal promoter of the project, cut the first turf. By June 1862, the sweating gangs of navvies had taken the track to Dingwall, the old Viking settlement of Thing Vall, their place of justice.

Work progressed more or less smoothly, apart from a serious delay caused by a recalcitrant laird, Mackenzie of Findon, who insisted upon a bridge rather than a level crossing at one point, to protect his tenants from the danger of rampaging locomotives.

In 1868, the line reached Golspie, where the company ran out of money. Golspie was the home of the Duke of Sutherland, one of the richest men in Europe and the largest shareholder in the enterprise.

The Duke financed the section of line between Golspie and Helmsdale, where he proposed to link it to the line being driven south by the Sutherland & Caithness Railway Company, in which he was also largest shareholder. The route, from a new exchange platform in Caithness at Georgemas Junction, was opened on 28 July 1874.

In September 1872, Queen Victoria travelled from Inverness to visit the Duke at Dunrobin Castle. In an extract from her diary, she recounts:

As our train proceeded, the scenery was lovely. Near the ruins of the old priory of Beauly, the river of the same name flows into the Beauly Firth and the firth looks like an enormous lake with hills rising above it, which were reflected on the perfectly still water.

At twenty minutes to four we reached Dingwall where there were Volunteers, as indeed there were everywhere, and where another address was presented and also flowers. Sir J. Matheson, Lord Lieutenant of the county, was named to me, also the Vice-Lieutenant, and some young ladies gave Beatrice nosegays.

After this and passing slowly through Tain and St Duthus (called after the Cathedral there), we thought that we would take our tea and coffee – which kept quite hot in the Norwegian kitchen – when suddenly, before we had finished, we stopped at Bonar Bridge and the Duke of Sutherland came up to the door.

He had been driving the engine (!) all the way from Inverness but only appeared now on account of this being the boundary of his territory, and the commencement of the Sutherland railroad. He expressed the honour it was to him that I was coming to Dunrobin.

The duchess took me to my rooms [in Dunrobin Castle], which had been purposely arranged and handsomely furnished by the dear late Duke and Duchess for us both ... I went to see Beatrice's room, which is close by, down three steps in the same passage. Fraulein Bauer, and Morgan, her dresser, are near her. Brown lives just opposite in the room intended for Albert's valet ... Dined at half-past eight alone in my sitting-room with Beatrice and Leopold, Brown waiting [her friend and gillie].

Today, board the train in Inverness. As you rumble north over Thomas Telford's Caledonian Canal, the next bridge crosses the River Beauly. Beaufort Castle, erstwhile home of Clan Fraser, is on your left. Beaufort was built on the ruins of Castle Downie, burned down in 1746 after the Battle of Culloden when the King's son, "Butcher Cumberland", ordered his soldiers to ravage the Highlands in reprisal for their support of Bonnie Prince Charlie's rebellion.

First stop is Muir of Ord, "The Moor of the Hammer", an old Highland cattle trading centre, where there used to be a branch line heading eastwards into the Black Isle and Fortrose. Ben Wyvis, a Munro (Scottish mountains over 914.4m in height), towers ahead, a graceful, rounded slope guarding the market town of Dingwall. Dingwall was the junction for Strathpeffer, a "spa" town in the nineteenth century famous for the healing quality of its water and still a popular holiday centre today.

North from Dingwall on Fyrish Hill is a monument erected by General Sir Hector Munro of Novar (1727–1805). Sir Hector distinguished himself at the Battle of Negapatam in India in 1781. When he returned home, to provide work for his impoverished tenants, he ordered a replica of the Gates of Negatapam to be built on the hill. The Gates are as much a memorial to the hardiness of the men who raised the massive stones as they are to Sir Hector.

The train ambles through Alness to Invergordon, the site of the last mutiny in the British Navy in 1931, now a centre for the repair of North Sea oil-drilling platforms and the Beatrice Oil Field Terminal. The line then passes Balnagown Castle, once the home of the powerful Ross family, now home to the controversial Al Fayed family who owned the London department store, Harrods.

Across the Dornoch Firth lies Skibo Castle, the Scottish home of Andrew Carnegie (1835–1918), the Dunfermline-born multimillionaire who built up the largest iron and steel business in America. Carnegie gifted more than £70 million to charitable works, including the building of libraries throughout the USA and in Scotland. Skibo is now the home of another multimillionaire, Peter de Savary, who runs it as an exclusive "retreat" for the world's rich and famous.

The track turns west at Tain to reach the Kyle of Sutherland and Strathcarron. This circuitous route was greatly influenced by the Duke of Sutherland. Since much of the line was to run through his land and because he was footing a large part of the bill, the route was designed to serve a two-fold purpose: communication with his sheep farms and ease of access to his sporting estates.

The Duke also insisted on a private station close to the gates of his Scottish residence, magnificent Dunrobin Castle. The Duke was determined to "improve" his estates. His tenants had to be taught the virtue of the Victorian work ethos, even if to do so meant evicting 16,000 of them from their farms and replacing them with sheep – the infamous Sutherland Clearances.

From Golspie through Brora to Helmsdale, the railway hugs the rugged Moray Firth coastline. It then turns north west up the Strath of Kildonan by the banks of the Helmsdale River, one of the most exclusive salmon streams in Scotland, much enjoyed by HRH Prince Charles and, in her earlier years, by his grandmother, HM The Queen Mother.

In the same year that the railway reached Golspie, Robert Gilchrist found gold in Helmsdale streams. Gilchrist had returned from the Australian gold fields and was convinced there was gold in his homeland hills. Thousands of people flocked north to seek their fortune.

Few found it, apart from the Duke. He owned the river and land and rented out forty-square-feet plots at a fee of £1 per month to prospectors. In the end, he made more money than most of the diggers. But when the presence of so many people began to affect his salmon fishing and deer stalking in 1870, the Duke closed the operation.

Midway up the strath, at Forsinard, the north line turns towards Caithness. There it crosses the Flow Country, one of the last great wilderness areas of Britain. This is a land of wide-open moors largely untouched by the hand of man for 7,000 years – until 1979. During a devastating decade,

200,000 acres of virgin moorland were planted with foreign conifers, simply so that those who did so could benefit financially from a tax loophole.

After what became known as "The Battle of the Flows", when conservationists fought the tax-dodgers, the madness ended. The Royal Society for the Protection of Birds (RSPB) purchased 30,000 acres of Flow Country and is working hard to undo the damage. The station building at Forsinard is their operational base, where there is an exhibition centre and RSPB staff lead guided walks into this magical land.

As the train leaves the Flow Country and enters Caithness, passengers stretch and sigh, collecting luggage and calming overexcited offspring. At Georgemas Junction, the train divides, one carriage going to Thurso, the other heading east by Loch Watten to Wick; the end of a long journey and, like my friend James Hamish Mackay, one that you will never forget.

28.
Unst Revisited

It was a good-to-be-alive morning. The Shetland sun shone on a sparkling bay as snow-white gulls wheeled and cried plaintively overhead. The sea was clear and calm, shaded silver, green and blue. Foam-tipped wavelets gently caressed the black rocks guarding the ruins of St Olaf's Church, built in the twelfth century on the foundations of an even earlier place of worship. St Olaf's sits on the cliff edge by the shore of Lunda Wick on the Island of Unst. Ann and I parked our car by the gaunt remains of Lund Hall and walked across the golden moor to have a few words with my ancestors.

Sandison has always been a pre-eminent name in the island and it is my belief that my people came from Unst, initially to Caithness, where my grandfather was born, and thence to Edinburgh where I was born. As ever in these northern climes, the force that drove many to move was the search for work. However, on the ferry over Bluemull Sound from Yell to Unst, the ticket-collector noted my name and remarked, "Well, be careful who you tell, that's all I'm saying." Clan Sandison must have gained a serious reputation, the cause of which remains unbeknown to me, but Sandisons still run one of Unst's longest-established businesses: Alexander Sandison & Sons, trading in Baltasound as Skibhoul Stores (tel: 01957 711304) and selling, well, just about everything.

Whatever, that morning, my ancestors were quiet enough in the space reserved for them in the graveyard at Lund. It is surrounded by a fence and presided over by a red marble memorial to Second Lieutenant Alexander Mundell Sandison, who died of wounds he received during the First World War. Other Sandisons keep him company and it was strange, standing there in the sunlight, contemplating my ultimate destination. Other tombstones reflect the important trading links Unst maintained with Northern Europe: the graves of two merchants from Bremen in Germany, Segedad Detken, who died in 1573, and Henrick Segelcken, who died in 1585. Another grave marks the last resting place of Thomas Mouat (1748–1819), the builder of Belmont House, near to where the ferry arrives and whom we will meet again later in our journey.

About thirty years ago, considerable anger was aroused when the UK government floated the idea of adjusting British Summer Time to bring it into line with European clocks, to make it easier for British companies to communicate by telephone with their counterparts on the continent. The prospect of everyone suffering considerable inconvenience for the benefit of a few created a storm of protest and the proposal was quietly abandoned. Recently, it has re-surfaced in a more user-friendly guise: the government, in their infinite wisdom, want to give us all a "present" of two extra hours of daylight. It is still nonsense, particularly in Unst, where it never really gets dark at all during summer months. For Unst, any alteration would mean almost perpetual daylight during summer and perpetual darkness in winter, and who wants that? Messrs Detken and Segelcken from Bremen seemed to communicate well enough in the sixteenth century without any disruption.

I am an angler and I discovered this truth in June 2009 when Davie McMillan, the president of the Unst Angling Club, asked me to join him and his members and guests at their annual "simmer dim" festival – the longest day, when anglers fish all through the night. It took me about a microsecond to say "yes" because, to me, returning to Unst is like coming home. The club was originally formed back in the 1960s and has always had a thriving membership. Indeed, as far back as 1733, when Thomas Gifford, the Laird of Busta on Mainland Shetland, visited Unst, he found that "the inhabitants are for the most part fishers. They have oxen, cows, some sheep, and plenty of little horses". Today, apart from the oxen, little has changed and fishing is an integral part of most people's activities. We started fishing at around 8pm and finished the following morning at 7am. It was quite wonderful, full of the sound of curlew, whimbrel and oyster-catcher and the happy splash of rising trout. Breakfast with a warming dram was also welcoming.

Unst is the most northern island in the Shetland archipelago and covers an area of some twenty by eight kilometres (117 square kilometres). It lies like a multi-coloured garnet stone, red, orange, violet, green and yellow, encompassed by endless ultramarine waves. Unst is hardly densely populated, being home to fewer than 700 souls, but it has some of the most beautiful and dramatic scenery on Planet Earth: wonderful white sand, near deserted beaches, wild moorlands carpeted with wild flowers, dramatic, seabird-clad cliffs that rise to a height of nearly 210m and the constant music of the sea. There is evidence of human habitation since Neolithic times 5,000 years ago and Unst has a tangled human history embracing many different peoples, from the Iron Age man, Picts and Vikings to the present day.

There are many reasons for spending time in Unst, not the least of which is the fact that it has two of Scotland's most significant National Nature Reserves in the north of the island: Keen of Hamar, near Baltasound on the east coast, and Hermaness, near Burrafirth on the west coast. Both reserves are carefully managed by Scottish Natural Heritage (SNH), the government-appointed body charged with the duty of preserving and protecting Scotland's precious natural environment. SNH describe Keen of Hamar as a lunar landscape, which at first sight seems to be bleak and lifeless, and yet it is home to some of the UK's rarest species of wildflower, including Edmondston's chickweed, slender St John's wort, kidney vetch, hoary whitlow grass and, one of my favourites, mountain everlasting.

The Hermaness reserve is an altogether wilder affair and properly exploring all that it has to offer will involve a vigorous walk; nothing too serious but you will need to be well-shod and clothed, and carry a compass and map and know how to use them. If you walk this way during the breeding season for bonxies, the Shetland name for the great skua, then it is advisable to take along a walking stick to fend off these large, aggressive birds as they crossly defend their nesting sites. But they are magnificent, as are the many thousands of other seabirds to be seen along the way: gannet, guillemot, black guillemot, Arctic skua, razorbill, kittiwake, fulmar, cormorant and puffin.

Start off from the car park at the end of the track that extends north from the B9086 road near Stackhoull, overlooking the battleground of Burra Firth – well, that is the old tale; the firth is enclosed by headlands: to the west, Hermaness (200m), and to the east, Saxa Vord (285m). Tradition has it that two giants lived there, Herman and Saxa, both of whom fell in love with a mermaid named Utsta. The rivals became so jealous of each other that they started chucking huge boulders across the firth, creating such a din that a local witch intervened. She buried Saxa beneath a cover of green grass and turned Herman into a cloud of mist.

Ann and I bumped into Herman during our first visit to the reserve; one moment it was bright and clear, and the next he had enveloped us in his clammy white cloak. With 150-metre cliffs only a step to the left, knifed by isolated stacks and ravine-like geos, we decided it was time for a pause, coffee and some serious compass and map work. Better safe than sorry. When the mist lifted, almost as quickly as it had descended, we found ourselves dangerously close to the cliff edge and sharing the sandy top with a gathering of firework-beaked tammie nories, the Shetland name for puffins.

That day, we also hoped to catch a glimpse of one of the most famous residents of Hermaness, Albert Ross, a black-browed albatross (*Thalassarche melanophrys*) that had strayed from its principal stronghold in the Falkland Islands and for many years visited Hermaness in search of a mate. Albert was first sighted in Scotland in 1967 in the Firth of Forth and for a few years returned regularly to, fruitlessly, court gannets on the Bass Rock. Unrequited in love, Albert then flew north and settled at Hermaness, but we found no sign of Albert. Unrequited again, he must have decided to hunt for love in pastures new.

We did, however, find the spectacular Muckle Flugga Lighthouse on its rocky pinnacle off the north coast of Hermaness between mainland Unst and Out Stack, the most northerly speck of UK territory. Muckle Flugga was begun in 1854 and completed in 1858, at a cost of £32,378 15s 5d (in old, pre-decimal currency). The lighthouse was built by Scottish lighthouse-builders extraordinaire Thomas and David Stevenson, father and uncle of another

Scottish hero of mine, the author Robert Louis Stevenson (RLS). It is claimed that RLS based the island in his book *Treasure Island* on the shape of Unst, a claim made for other islands, but I am sure that Unst has that honour given the remarkable similarity of Unst to the map that appears in the novel.

A sadder story is recounted about Out Stack. Lady Jane Franklin, wife of the Arctic explorer Sir John – who perished in 1845 during a search for the fabled North West Passage – came to Unst seeking help. The incident is recounted in P.N. Guy's excellent book *The Island of Unst* and is based upon information provided by Jessie Saxby: "When Lady Franklin was wandering over Britain in eager quest for men to search for Sir John and his companions, she came to Unst and asked to be taken to the most northerly spot where she could look over the sea and – as she said –"send love on wings of prayer" to the ill-fated adventurer. The weather chanced to be exceptionally fine and my father, with a picked crew, took Lady Franklin to set foot on Ootsta [Out Stack]. Those who were there said she stood for some minutes on the somber rock, quite silent, tears falling slowly, and her hands stretched out towards the north."

Whilst much of the glory of Unst is undoubtedly founded on its landscape and history, the island is also famous for the welcome it gives to visitors amongst the many events, activities and community projects that are organised throughout the year. Indeed, it is probably fair to say that on every day of every month on the island "something" is happening "somewhere". A good start-point is the Uyeasound Up Helly Aa, held in the first week of February. The event celebrates Shetland's links with its Viking ancestors, for until 1468, Shetland was a province of Norway; in that year, King Christian I of Norway pledged the islands to King James III of Scotland as part of the dowry when James married Christian's daughter, Margaret. The money was never paid and, thus, in 1471, Shetland became part of Scotland.

Similar to the festival held in Lerwick, discussed in Chapter 13, throughout the year, a replica of a Viking galley is built and carefully fitted out. It is in itself a work of art but destined to be destroyed by fire during the Uyeasound Up Helly Aa. Teams of local men, Guizers, one hundred-strong, and their leader, the Guizer Jarl, carrying burning torches, march in procession through the town and set the galley ablaze. Be warned, however, that the parties that follow can last for several days. During the months preceding the ceremony, visitors to Unst may visit the shed were the galley is being built and hear about the traditions of the Up Helly Aa, and see the wondrously decorated galley name plates from past occasions.

Further north, in July, is the Baltasound Regatta, the most northerly such regatta in the UK. There are races throughout the day, hotly disputed by crews from other Shetland isles, Yell and Whalsay. Landlubbers are also well-catered for, with activities for children, games and a beer tent for those so disposed, which features the famous Valhalla brew, made at, yes, you've guessed it, the most northerly brewery in UK. The day ends with an evening of entertainment provided by local musicians, fiddlers, accordion players and singers. Nearby, at Saxa Vord, a former Royal Air Force station, visitors can also enjoy superb food at the Saxa Vord Restaurant, based essentially on local produce. The restaurant was a finalist in the 2010 Highlands and Islands "Dining Out Experience" Tourist Awards. And for something simple, but none-the-less excellent, don't miss out on the Chip Suppers which are regularly held in Baltasound Village Hall.

If you have an interest in boats, then head for the Unst Boat Haven, part of the Unst Heritage Trust and dedicated to the maritime history of Shetland boats – all traditionally built for use under sail or oar, double ended and clinker built using a construction method that dates back for more than 1,700 years. They are supremely beautiful. The Haven has seventeen boats, including a nineteenth-century sixareen, rowed by a crew of six, with a square sail for use when the weather was suitable. These boats, which could be nine metres in length, were used for off-shore fishing to a distance of forty miles. The love between a Shetland man and his boat is indivisible. I remember talking to a friend of mine about this "affair". He told me, "Bruce, in Shetland you may do as you please with another man's girlfriend or wife, but you must never, ever, touch his boat."

We now return to Belmont House, near the ferry terminal and built by

Thomas Mouat, son of the Lairg of Garth, whom, you will recall, lies asleep along with my Sandison ancestors in the little graveyard overlooking the sea at Lunda Wick. Before deciding on what Belmont would look like, Thomas visited a number of notable houses near Edinburgh and eventually decided on a Georgian-style dwelling, and in doing so, created an almost perfect example of this design. His family lived there until well into the twentieth century, when the house became derelict. Historic Scotland describes Belmont thus: "As well as being the most ambitious house in the north isles, Belmont is Shetland's least altered classical mansion, its interior being a particularly remarkable survival."

The old house was rescued by the vision and hard work of the Belmont Trust, an independent body with five trustees who purchased the property in 1996 from Edinburgh architect John Hope for just £5. Since then, the trust, with their contractors, The Shetland Amenity Trust, has spent upwards of £1.2 million restoring Belmont to its former glory. The restoration was carried out by unpaid volunteers and specialist contractors were employed when required. I spoke to one of those involved, Wendy Scott, and she confessed that when they began the project, they had no idea exactly how much time and effort would have to be put into the project to bring it to fruition.

Mark Finnie, architect and trustee, has been faithful to the Georgian style of the building: "The drawing room paint is exactly the same as the original colour, wooden floors with oriental rugs and stone flags outside to form paths in the forecourt." The end result is of enormous credit to all involved. Belmont House has taken on a renewed lease of life as a fully-restored Georgian country house sleeping up to twelve people "in a stylish interior for holidays" and will also be used as a venue for weddings, meetings, and art and community events (see http://www.belmontunst.org.uk for details).

For more information on Unst, you could do no better than try to obtain a copy of *Unst, My Island Home and Its Story* by a namesake of mine, Charles Sandison. The author lived at Hammar in Unst and finished the book in January 1966. It is out of print now but Amazon or Abe Books should have copies. The ISBN is 978-0900662003 and the volume was published by

Shetland Times Ltd in 1968. Sandison captured the true worth of Unst in a fine poem, 'The Island's Call':

> To Unst, its high and rock-bound shore,
> And smiling summer bays,
> Its glorious sun and wind and sea,
> And joyous springtime days.
>
> The lapping water between the weed
> When the tide is on the make,
> And the eiderduck with her brood of young
> Scurrying in her wake.
>
> The freedom of bright and long days spent
> In row-boat and in sail,
> The downward swoop of the gannet,
> And the loom of the finner whale.
>
> I will leave the town with its bustling crowds,
> Its one-way streets and all,
> And will hie me away to a northern isles
> For I hear its magic call.

However, perhaps I should leave the last words to another remarkable Scotsman, Sir John Sinclair of Lybster in Caithness, who published his *Statistical Account of Scotland for 1791–1800*. He commented about life in Shetland in the 1790s: "People frank and open in their manners, bold, hardy and humane. Music and dancing are very favoured in winter. Many common people play with skill on the violin." More than two hundred years later, you will find that this is still true. And, I am sure you will also find a goodly number of Sandisons amongst that happy breed.

29.
Cawdor Castle

Every year a Shakespeare play is performed in front of the drawbridge of Cawdor Castle to the east of the City of Inverness. The summer of 2011 featured his wonderful comedy *Twelfth Night*. Cawdor Castle is one of Scotland's oldest and most glorious buildings and has sheltered generations of the same family for more than 600 years. Before the performance, guests picnicked in the Flower Garden and then sat upon the lawn amidst the sweet scent of summer to listen to the tale of mistaken identity and unrequited love. In 1370, more than 200 years before Shakespeare wrote the work, William, 3rd Thane of Cawdor, started work on his new castle and now, people can gather at Cawdor to enjoy both the castle and Shakespeare's plays.

Prior to the building of the present-day castle, the family occupied a smaller castle nearby, probably a defensive fort, about a mile north east of Cawdor and built on an artificial hillock amidst marshy ground. When William made the decision to build the new residence, he decided that the site should be chosen by chance, rather than by design. He is said to have packed gold into a coffer and strapped it to the back of a donkey, then set the animal off to wander where it would. Clearly, the progress of the donkey was closely monitored by William and eventually, at nightfall, the beast settled by a tree on a rocky outcrop where there was a source of water – an excellent building site with a good supply of drinking water and firm foundations for a castle. Thus, William believed, the Cawdor family would be "forever prosperous".

Cawdor Castle is famous for its association with Shakespeare. In his "Scottish play", *Macbeth*, the bard has King Duncan being murdered at Cawdor by Macbeth, then Thane of Cawdor. In fact, Duncan was wounded in a battle at Pitgaveny in 1040 and died at Elgin Castle some miles to the east of Cawdor. Also, given that Cawdor Castle was not built until the late fourteenth century, it is entirely impossible that Duncan could have been murdered there. However, Shakespeare never allowed uncomfortable truths to intrude upon his construction of a good tale, so the myth persists to this day, much to the amusement and pleasure of visitors to the castle.

My own visit to Cawdor occurred in December 2010 on a sparkling morning with Christmas knocking on the door. I was to meet Gräfin Angelika Lažanský von Bukowa, Dowager Countess of Cawdor and widow of Hugh, the 24th Thane. My instructions were precise: "Arrive at 11.30am, enter by the exit, park under the trees and someone will meet you on the drawbridge." I confess that I was intimidated. I was well aware of the link between Cawdor and *Macbeth* and would not have been in the least bit startled to catch a glimpse of three witches brewing up something unwholesome on the bleak moor as I passed by. But what if I arrived late? Would I be bundled unceremoniously into a dungeon to weep and wail, chained to a dank wall? These worries are probably why I got lost, which is hard to do in a tiny place like Cawdor Village.

With time running out, I asked directions from two men in a van. They looked strangely at each other: "Do you see these pillars on the other side of the road?" the driver asked.

"You mean the ones that have a sign on them saying 'EXIT'?"

"Yes," he replied. "Just go through there and follow the road to the castle."

With that, he wound up the window of the van and, still shaking his head in disbelief, drove off. I glanced at my watch, a minute remaining, and shot up the road as fast as I could safely go. Suddenly, there were the trees and the old castle and, thank the lord, the drawbridge, which I was pleased to note was in the lowered position. Grabbing what little was left of my dignity, I hurried to the drawbridge.

Shortly thereafter, I was courteously welcomed by a strikingly handsome woman accompanied by two border terriers. Lady Cawdor settled me in a comfortable chair in her study and took her place behind a large, well-ordered desk. A log fire sparked and crackled in the grate, filling the small room with warmth and the unforgettable scent of wood smoke. I explained again the purpose of my visit and began by asking her about the story of the donkey, the gold and the tree. Was it fact or fiction?

She said, "That is obviously a family legend but my husband, who was someone who liked fact rather than fancy, complained that he couldn't possibly tell the tale to unsuspecting visitors without some evidential proof. On the ground floor of the castle there are the remains of a fossilized tree – I will show you in a moment. He chopped off a bit of wood from the tree and had it analyzed by carbon dating. The answer came back that the tree was alive in 1372, plus or minus forty-five years. Now, this tree is exactly in the middle of the central structure of the castle, exactly opposite the drawbridge and there is no doubt that the original tower was built over the tree."

For years, the family thought that the tree was a hawthorn, which is not surprising; Hugh Fife, in his wonderful book about native Highland trees, *Warriors and Guardians*, notes that "the belief that this tree [hawthorn] has a strong affinity of things beyond the obvious world has persisted for thousands of years. There also appears to be some special link between the tree and hereditary chiefs." Fife also incorrectly identified the Cawdor tree as being a hawthorn: "At another location in the North East Highlands," he said, "a very famous castle was built over a hawthorn tree and some centuries later, the tree was still alive in the building's cellar."

The inquiring mind of the 24th Thane and modern technology resolved the issue of the true identity of the tree: it was not hawthorn but holly. This discovery gave considerably more credence to the story about William, the gold and the donkey, in as much as holly, in Gaelic culture, was considered to be a "protective" tree and, like other evergreens, had the power to ward off evil spirits. Yes, indeed, just the right place to build the castle to ensure that he and his descendants would be "forever prosperous".

Nevertheless, the word "prosperous" can have different meanings to different people: to turn out well, success, good fortune, health, wealth, happiness, thriving. So I asked Lady Cawdor what she thought the previous

Thanes, looking at the castle today, would think about Cawdor and if they would agree that the family had been "forever prosperous". She thought about this for a moment, looking down for guidance at the younger of the two border terriers, which was comfortably ensconced on her lap.

"I think that I would take that as meaning that the family, in a long line, continued here. The statement, in that sense, to prosper, seems to me to mean to continue, rather than in any monetary terms. And, considering the history of Scotland during that period, the early and middle-ages, it was indeed good fortune that the family did survive, in a direct line, during these often bloody times," she answered.

Few would doubt the veracity of Lady Cawdor's statement. The family lived through some of the most turbulent events in our history: the Scottish Wars of Independence, Henry VIII's "Rough Wooing" of our realm and the turmoil of the Reformation; the bloodshed and mayhem of religious wars; the death of Mary of Guise (1560), mother of Mary, Queen of Scots, which left Scotland in a state of civil war; Oliver Cromwell's tenure, when Cawdor was one of the few Scottish castles that he did not "knock about a bit"; the Jacobite Rebellions of 1689, 1715 and 1745.

However, towards the end of the seventeenth century and in spite of the uncertainty of these times, Hugh, the 14th Thane, embarked upon an ambitious programme designed to alter the character of Cawdor from fortress to family home; a good idea given that he had nine children aged from four to twenty-one and a numerous household, including the chaplain, the gentleman, the butler, the cook, the cook's man, the porter, the coachman, two footmen, two gentlewomen, the chamber maid, three byrewomen and a dairy maid – twenty-seven people in all. The work was completed to Hugh's satisfaction in 1702 and Cawdor, as it is today, is very much his legacy to the family home.

When Hugh died in 1716, his successor, his grandson John, moved the family south to live in London and on the family estates in Wales; a custom subsequently adopted by many of his peers, when, after centuries, the Lairds essentially abandoned their Highland clans; thus paving the way for the savage clearances of the nineteenth century when the descendants of these Lairds chose to populate their Scottish estates with sheep, rather than with people. Cawdor Castle was left, unchanged, and cared for by a succession of factors, employed to do so by Cawdor Estates.

Lady Cawdor cares for the castle today, with support and help from a small staff of key helpers: Martin Nelson, Lady Cawdor's chef, who has been with her for twenty-seven years; Alison Clark, her assistant in the tourism office, who has worked there for twenty-eight years; Derek Hosie, the head gardener, who has nurtured the famous Cawdor Gardens for nearly thirty years. In all, there are fourteen full-time members on Lady Cawdor's management team, along with seasonal staff numbering fifty-four, mostly from Cawdor and the surrounding area. The castle is open seven days a week from 1 May until the first Sunday in October and attracts upwards of 80,000 visitors each year.

Gardening has always been a passion with Lady Cawdor, clearly reflected in the three principal gardens adjacent to the castle: the Flower Garden, Old Walled Garden and the Wild Garden. I asked about her special interest in the gardens and she told me: "I love gardens. And the great fortune is that I have this excellent head gardener who has been here, as I say, twenty-nine years. We have done a lot of work in the gardens. The most recent is that we have created a slate garden, with some of the old slates when we replaced slates on the roof of the castle. We redid a small area of the flower garden, with a beautiful fountain made out of slate in the middle, a lovely grey colour. The slates came from a quarry near Elgin 250 years ago, the last time the castle was reroofed.

"We are completely organic here. My vegetable gardens, my summer and winter vegetable gardens, have been organic for thirty-one years. That is my major passion, well, one of them. We grow all our own vegetables. In the summer, a lot of those go to our restaurant for the benefit of the visitors. We are self-sufficient, except for milk and butter, and olive oil, of course. But basically, self-sufficient; we have salmon in the river, partridge, grouse, pheasant, hare and roe deer – you can't really ask for more."

Lady Cawdor fiercely guards the integrity of organic farming in the area and, in 2002, played a leading role in opposing the trial-plantings of genetically modified crops near the castle because of uncertainty about the impact these crops might have on crops produced by organic farmers. She managed to have two of the trials stopped but a third trial, on Roskill Farm near Munlochy, across the Moray Firth on the Black Isle, went ahead. The public debate she organised was attended by 350 people, with many more being turned away because of lack of space.

Since then, she has continued her support for organic farming and told me, "For five or six years now we have held a 'Living Food' day on the last Saturday in September. We invite all the good organic producers in the Highlands to join us and there are usually about forty to fifty different stalls. Last year, we had over 2,000 visitors during the day. It is an excellent showcase for the wonderful produce of the Highlands. I really do think, as far as food is concerned, that we produce some of the best raw materials in the world."

With that, Lady Cawdor conducted me on a tour of the principal rooms in the Castle: the drawing room with its wonderful paintings, including works by Sir Joshua Reynolds, Sawrey Gilpin, Thomas Lawrence and Frederick Say; the Tapestry Bedroom with its magnificent Venetian headboard on the four-poster marriage-bed of Sir Hugh Campbell, the 14th Thane of Cawdor and Lady Henrietta Stuart, wed in 1662, and the lovely Flemish tapestries purchased in 1682 at a total cost of £483, including £3 customs duty; the Woodcock Room, Pink Bedroom, Pink Dressing Room, Tower Room and, finally, the Thorn Tree Room with the famous fossilized holly, over which the castle was built.

Hugh, the 24th Thane and 6th Earl Cawdor, who died in 1993, left a splendid and detailed account of all the furnishings, ornaments and artifacts in the castle. You will find this at the back of the guide book to Cawdor, which was also written by Hugh. Both are highly entertaining and absolutely essential if you are to get the most out of your visit to the castle. I have visited quite a few castles in my time, carefully reading the attendant literature. Invariably, it is, more often than not, as dry as dust. Hugh's writing is a perfect example of how such subjects should be tackled: fact-packed but with a liberal sprinkling of fun and good humour.

I had asked Lady Cawdor what the previous Thanes would have thought about the present status of the castle and I wondered how she felt about the future – would the family continue to prosper? "Cawdor Estate is a very large entity. The Castle and the land that belongs with the castle is very much part of that. The Castle and the Estate are run in two different ways. The whole thing is 58,000 acres. My stepson, Colin Cawdor, [the 25th Thane and 7th Earl of Cawdor] runs a very good shoot and we have a beautiful grouse moor. We have an excellent partridge shoot, pheasant shoot and, of course, salmon fishing on the River Findhorn. The Estate has a formal factor; I have a general manager. As to the future, well, the next generation is very much alive and well, which is my stepson and he also has a son, so as far as I can look down the line, I think that everything will be all right."

But before I left, I had one final question to ask Lady Cawdor: what did the castle mean to her? "What it means to me is that I am the current guardian thereof and that is what my husband wanted me to do, which is why he left it to me. I am just a link in a very long chain and although it belongs to me, it is really the other way round – I belong to it. I do my very best to look after it, like an old relation really. An old house is very much a being in its own right. I just see myself as the guardian now," was her reply.

As I drove home, I thought to myself, "Well, an old house it may be but it could not have a more caring and committed guardian," whilst making a careful note of the date 23 July, Cawdor Castle, *Twelfth Night*, and keeping a weather eye open for witches along the way.

For full details about the castle and annual events, contact: Cawdor Castle Ltd, Cawdor Castle, Nairn, Scotland IV12 5RD; Tel: 01667 404401; Fax: 01667 404674; Website: http://www.cawdorcastle.com; Email: info@cawdorcastle.com

30.
Alladale Wilderness Lodge and Reserve

Little of lasting worth in this world has ever been achieved without passion and commitment. Governments – well, some governments – in their various ways, seek to do so but all of the available evidence seems to indicate that, for much of the time, they labour in vain. Nowhere is this more self-evident than in the field of conservation: our environment is continually under pressure from commercial interests, the rape of our seas, the destruction of native forests, industrial pollution, profit before probity. A Cree Indian prophecy encapsulates this belief: "Only after the last tree has been cut down / Only after the last river has been poisoned / Only after the last fish has been caught / Only then will you find that money cannot be eaten."

Happily, there are people, individuals, who are prepared to accept these challenges and to confront these issues. Mostly, they are personally wealthy and prepared to give of their time and money to try to restore degraded parts of Planet Earth to their natural state. And, of course, there are many others, less enriched, who toil in the same way as best as they can. But they all have one thing in common: an enhanced desire to leave nothing behind for future generations other than the friendly imprint of their care for the land that gives us all life. This is the story of one such project in the Highlands of Scotland, a story that is just beginning.

The announcement a few years ago that the Alladale Wildlife Reserve proposed to reintroduce wolves, lynx, bison, brown bear and elk to the Highlands was met with mixed feelings. The Scottish Mountaineering Council, Ramblers Association and the Mountain Bothy Association all launched fierce attacks on the proposals because, they insist, the building of fences will restrict access to the hills. The Highland Council, Scottish Government, Scottish Natural Heritage, *et al* also expressed concern. Neighbouring estates have expressed alarm about the reduction of the Alladale red deer population and how such a reduction will impact upon their deer.

As such, this response was similar to the public response that has greeted other schemes; most recently, the reintroduction of white-tailed eagles, commonly known as sea eagles – great raptors that were driven to extinction in Scotland in the early years of the twentieth century – and the reintroduction of European beavers, a species that has been absent from Scotland since the seventeenth century.

In spite of predictions that life in Caledonia as we know it would come to an immediate end if the sea eagles and beavers arrived, they are here; sea eagles in Mull and Sutherland and other areas of the north, and beavers in the Knapdale Forest in Argyll. The sea eagles are doing well, thriving mightily, and they delight thousands of visitors and local people every year. The beavers have settled in comfortably, thank you, and are busy building their lodges and getting on with what nature intended for them, propagating their kind.

As far as I can judge, the prophets of doom have been confounded. The sun still rises from the east each morning and still sets in the west at the end of each day. But the doubters persist in their complaints: allegedly, sea eagles kill and eat hundreds of lambs and sheep each year and the beavers severely disrupt riverine habitats and wild fish stocks with their tree-felling and dam-building proclivities. There is only anecdotal evidence to support such claims but they continue to exercise the minds of many of those opposed to any form of radical change.

Such complaints are nothing new amidst Scotland's wild lands. Any creature that is perceived to be a threat to the inalienable right of humans to make a profit, regardless of collateral damage, goes on to many land-owner's and land-worker's hit lists: sea eagle, golden eagle, buzzard, hen harrier, cormorant, goosander, merganser, heron, otter, seals, and, at least until the Land Reform (Scotland) Act was passed in 2003, in extreme cases, climbers, hill walkers, ramblers, bird watchers *et al*.

This is the historical background against which the reintroduction of wolves, lynx, bison, brown bear and elk has to be viewed. Those who express concern about these matters have the right to be fairly heard. Scotland's legal freedom-to-roam legislation has been hard won and has to be vigorously protected. Those who propose these reintroductions will always fail in their aim to do so unless they obtain the support of our political masters, the general public and the majority of the local communities upon which the proposals will impact. It is right and proper that this is the case; after all, we live in a democracy.

Mr Paul Lister, co-founder of the MFI furniture chain, is the owner and leading visionary of the 23,000-acre Alladale Wildlife Reserve, about forty miles north from Inverness, the capital city of the Highlands. He is a passionate conservationist and the driving force behind the proposed reintroductions described above. Paul Lister is also the founder of The European Nature Trust (TENT), an organisation committed to the protection and restoration of threatened wilderness areas, wild habitats and the wildlife living within them.

Hugh Fullerton-Smith, for five years general manager at Alladale, is every bit as passionate and committed to the concept of conservation as is Paul Lister and he has recently been appointed as director of TENT. Fullerton-Smith has extensive experience of conservation issues throughout the world: in the UK, USA, Mongolia and in the Carpathian Mountains, across Romania, Ukraine, Poland, Slovakia, the Czech Republic and Hungry where TENT is seeking philanthropic and institutional funding to safeguard large tracts of forest and other wild areas.

I set off early one morning in August to find out exactly what was going on at Alladale and why it had raised the hackles of so many of our fellow Scots. Alladale lies at the heart of Clan Ross country and bestrides the boundary between Sutherland and Ross-shire. It has a considerable history of angst, most known for the little church at Croick, a few miles to the west of Ardgay at the head of the Dornoch Firth. This provided shelter for the people of Glencalvie, part of the Alladale lands, when they were evicted from their homes in 1845 to make way for sheep. About ninety souls, destitute men, women and children, huddled in the churchyard under plaids and blankets.

They engraved sad messages on the windows of the church: "Glencalvie people was in the churchyard here on 24 May 1845." "Glencalvie tenants residing here." "Glencalvie people, the wicked generation." Many of those evicted had been told by their ministers, appointed by the Lairds conducting the clearances, that they were being evicted because of their sins before God, although those so-called sins were never detailed. All that was required of those whose ancestors had lived and toiled the land for generations was to immediately pack whatever they could carry and go.

Today, this area is very much the sporting and recreational paradise of southern owners and their guests. My friend Mike and I drove past their lodges, Gruinards, Amat and Glencalvie, and then followed the blue ribbon of the River Carron through magnificent forests of ancient Scots Pine up a small hill to Alladale Lodge. The great house is splendidly set amidst well-tended lawns and fine gardens. Having announced our arrival, we were welcomed by the reserve manager, Innes MacNeill, a sparse, strikingly fit young man with a natural air of command and common sense. His experience spans almost twenty years of habitat management, flora and fauna on the reserve. We sat round the dining room table over coffee and home-made shortbread whilst Innes outlined his plan for our day on the reserve.

The key question in my mind was to determine the position in regard to the reintroduction of the major predators: wolves and brown bears. Personally, I harbour doubts about doing so. Not because I think that it is in any way wrong, but rather my concern that these animals would be persecuted today as much as they were persecuted when they naturally roamed these lands. It became clear that Paul Lister and his team could not proceed with the reintroductions until such time as they were certain that the habitat provided was sufficiently large to safely sustain them.

Alladale extends to 23,000 acres but to establish an area large enough to safely accommodate two small packs of wolves requires a minimum 50,000 acres. This means that either Alladale's neighbours have to be persuaded to sign up to the proposal or that Alladale will have to try to buy adjacent land on the open market if and when it becomes available. Until these conditions are met, the reintroduction remains uncertain.

With Innes at the wheel of a Reserve Land Rover, we set off along the bumpy road leading up Gleann Mór into the Glencalvie Forest, centred by a white, rocky, tumbling stream, the Abhainn á Ghlinne Mhóir. Although there are no Munros on the Reserve, the hills are considerable and majestic: to the south, the long ridge of Dunach Liath (554m), Dunna Liath (690m) and Carn Feur-lochain (694m), to the north Sron Gun Aran (622m) and An Socach (745m). These hills are scattered with wild brown trout lochs that delight anglers: Crom, Sgeireach, little Lochan nam Breac Buidh, Pollaig, Lochan nan Leac and na Gabhalach Nodha, full of hard-fighting fish.

Innes commented, "Man has destroyed the glens, not the deer or the sheep, but man. He cut down the trees and burned the ground. Any young saplings that have tried to come through during the past 200 years, the sheep and deer have had them. Putting it back is a tall order for us and we are trying to replant areas. It is great to think that the trees will self regenerate, but they will not, because of sheep and deer, this why we have to move in and help."

The hills host a wide range of wildlife, including purple swaths of bell heather, stands of Scots pine, amidst newly planted trees of the same species, cautious ptarmigan on the high tops, red grouse, the great raptors, golden eagle, buzzard, peregrine, kestrel, delicate merlin and vast, coal-black raven. By the river and on the lower slopes, you will find otter, fox, pine marten and badger. Throughout the reserve, red deer abound. This is the largest mammal in Britain and it has survived in some form or other since time immemorial. Currently, there is a population of some 1,000 red deer on the reserve, although numbers have been reduced to allow the natural regeneration on both old and newly planted forests.

The reserve's commitment to the re-establishment of the old forest is total. I asked Innes how many trees had been planted in recent years and he told me, "From 1992 until 2011, upwards of 500,000 native trees will have been planted. Rowan and birch are quickly established, the Scots pine are much slower. We have designed open plan thickets and natural scatterings. The hill crests are planted with pine and we think, and hope, that it looks like how it possibly did look in the past. After fifteen years, it is safe to take down the fence that has protected them from predation by deer – there are no longer sheep on the reserve. All the species we plant here are native to this region. We are just about to start planting 67,000 trees in this area; mainly pine but birch, rowan, holly, willow, juniper, alder and aspen as well. This is long-term work. We won't see the result but future generations will, and they will benefit from doing so. It's a 100-year restoration project."

Half way up the glen, we stopped to say good morning to the reserve's five Highland ponies, two of which are used to bring in stalked deer, the others taking visitors on adventure treks through the hills. That morning, two of the beautiful beasts were being saddled by John Calder, who looks after them for the reserve, and a lady guest accompanied by her boisterous, talkative dog, Reah. We next stopped at a wonderful badger hide, carefully disguised into the side of a small hillock overlooking the stream. Innes pointed out the set, on the far bank, where the badgers had been busy, house-keeping, clearing out unwanted earth from their home. We were also introduced to the reserve's wild boar colony, curious animals that ran down the hill to greet us. We were similarly introduced to Hercules and Hulda, elk brought onto the reserve recently. They are designated as being dangerous wild animals and are safely contained within a considerable area of ground, but they were friendly enough when we said hello.

The reserve also provides, in conjunction with the Challenger Trust programme, wonderful opportunities for young people to become involved in the work of the reserve. The Challenger Trust is a registered charity and Alladale runs a "challenge", funded by the Young People's Fund for Scotland and the Lister Charitable Trust. It provides facilities for twenty-four young people to take part in development adventure activities whilst working with rangers on conservation projects and helping with running the reserve, building self-confidence and learning new skills.

The Alladale Challenge starts on Monday mornings and finishes the following Friday evening, during April, May and June. Innes explained some of the tasks the boys and girls are set: "They recently helped plant about 2,000 trees in the boar's compound. The children and their teachers camp out and love it. They come from a catchment area of within forty miles of Alladale and, currently, six high schools are involved: they undertake tree planting, tree surveys, pulling down fences, guided wildlife walks and talks, fly fishing on the river, abseiling, team leadership skills and route finding."

The Alladale Reserve also supports twenty full- and part-time jobs in an area where employment opportunities are limited. The reserve has its own saw mill and much of the furniture that adorns the reserve properties is made from their own wood, in their own workshop; designed and built by the reserve handyman, Blair Barnet. Alladale generates much of its own electricity from water power and up to 70% comes from this source, depending upon water levels in the rivers.

Clearly, the capital investment in setting up and developing the Alladale Wilderness Lodge and Reserve has been considerable and, as such, it also has to generate income to sustain that development. Alladale Lodge and the reserve properties provide that source of income. The Lodge and the luxurious self-catering "bothies" are available to rent and are increasingly well patronised. Those with the means to do so enjoy a standard of accommodation and service that is beyond excellent and many have become regular Alladale guests, experiencing all that is finest in Scottish scenery and hospitality.

They are also exposed to the passion and commitment to the environment that Paul Lister and his team have brought to their dream of returning a degraded part of the Highland landscape to its rightful former glory. I, for one, welcome this commitment. As to reintroducing wolves, brown bear and lynx, I also hope that this dream becomes a reality. Only time and the continued passion of people like Paul Lister can make it happen.

For further information, contact: Alladale Wilderness Lodge & Reserve, Ardgay, Sutherland, Scotland IV24 3BS; Tel: 01863 755338; Fax: 01863 755352; Email: reservations@alladale.com; Website: www.alladale.com

31.
Ardtornish, a Dream in the West

Morvern and Ardtornish in the West Highlands of Scotland is one of the least visited and yet most beautiful areas of the land I love. It retains a sense of peace often lacking amidst Caledonia's more popular airts. Even today there is no easy way into this magnificent wilderness. The best route is by the short ferry crossing over Loch Linnhe at the Corran Narrows, eight miles south from Fort William. But you will still be gripped in the embrace of a tortuous, single-track road for the last part of your journey, climbing from shores of Loch Sunart between Beinn nam Beathrach (582m) and Taobh Dubh (352m) before descending to the sea through the glory of Gleann Geal, the White Glen of Morvern.

I became interested in the area after reading Philip Gaskell's book, *Morvern Transformed: A Highland Parish in the Nineteenth Century*, and, particularly, coming from North Sutherland, by the infamous Patrick Sellar's association with Ardtornish. In 1838, Sellar – who had been an agent of the Duke of Sutherland and personally oversaw the brutal Strathnaver Clearances between 1813 and 1819 – acquired 6,810 acres of land around Loch Arienas and brought sheep down from his Sutherland estates. Clearances soon followed. Forty-four families amounting to 230 people were immediately evicted.

Eventually, Sellar had control of upwards of 30,000 Morvern acres and he settled himself in the original Ardtornish House, once the home of the Duke of Argyll's factor. This grand building stood on a high promontory jutting out into the Sound of Mull, close to the ruins of Ardtornish Castle; a tumble of broken walls with a stubby tower clinging to the edge of gull-cry-filled cliffs that look west over the sea to the Island of Mull.

I walked out to the castle with young Russell MacIntyre, the Ardtornish Estate acting visitor manager, and we talked about those who had lived there down the ages – from the earliest Mesolithic people, Neolithic man, Celts, Picts, Vikings and Highlanders – and the struggles they must have endured to survive in such an inhospitable environment. Sellar's home, like the castle, is now in ruins. The few remaining walls and arches are moss-covered and almost invisible amidst the tangle of branches and bushes that have invaded the remains of the great man's residence.

John Macdonald was one of the casualties of the clearances and, as an old man, he was appointed spokesman for the community when, in 1883, the Napier Commission came north to take evidence about these sad events. At a meeting in the Free Church Hall at Lochaline, he was asked by the Commission what he wanted and he replied: "I would like it to be the way it was before, if it were possible, that is. I should like to have a croft and my cows back again, as before."

After the clearances, two men owned most of the land in Morvern: Patrick Sellar, who had Ardtronish Estate, and his neighbour, Octavius Smith, who had made his fortune distilling and selling gin in Victorian London and owned Achranich Estate. Smith's family built the present day Ardtornish House, a vast, imposing Victorian mansion.

But the Achranich Estate lay between Sellar's land and the men were soon at loggerheads. The dispute centered on salmon fishing rights in the River Aline. Although Smith owned one bank of the stream, Sellar had the sole rights to fishing. As relations deteriorated, Sellar refused Smith permission to fish and Smith responded by denying Sellar access across his land to tend to his business at Loch Arienas.

The matter was placed in the hands of their respective lawyers and the young families of the stubborn adults were ordered, on pain of severe retribution, to ignore each other. Happily, however, before the dispute came to court, it was resolved; Sellar agreed to sell half of his fishing rights to Smith, whilst Smith agreed to give Sellar a right of way across his land. Thus, Victorian propriety and honour was satisfied and thereafter the two families lived amicably together. Eleanor Sellar later recalled, "I remember Gertrude, Mr Smith's youngest daughter, telling me how the new peace was inaugurated by her mother and herself, then a child of eight, lunching at Ardtornish. Mr Sellar set her beside himself and called her his little lady. The goings to and from between the two places was as perpetual as they had been strictly forbidden the year before."

In time, the families were united by marriage and the estates merged into what is now Ardtornish Estate and, because of Queen Victoria's love of all things Scottish, the great and good flocked to the Highlands, to walk, fish, hunt stags and generally disport themselves far from the madding crowd. Ardtornish welcomed many famous visitors, including, in 1853, Alfred Lord Tennyson, poet laureate, accompanied by his friend and fellow poet, Francis Turner Palgrave of *Golden Treasury* fame. Their host was Patrick Sellar's son and heir, William, Professor of Humanities at Edinburgh University. Although Tennyson and Palgrave had intended to visit Loch Coruisk in Skye, they were so captivated by Ardtornish that they decided to stay there. Tennyson later wrote, "For though he missed a day in Skye / He spent a day in heaven."

John Buchan, statesman, soldier, author, poet and angler, met Gerard Craig Sellar, Patrick's grandson, in South Africa in 1902 and he and his wife regularly visited Ardtornish. Indeed, Buchan probably conceived the idea for his marvelous book *John Macnab* from the earlier dispute between Smith and Sellar. The story is based upon a public challenge to poach a deer and a salmon from a neighbour's land, on a given day, without the participants being caught. Buchan dedicated his book to Rosalind Maitland, Craig Sellar's sister.

When I last visited Ardtornish in March 2010 the estate provided me with comfortable accommodation in a cottage by the river. The estate has a number of excellent self-catering properties where guests can enjoy a fulfilling holiday amongst wonderful scenery. Not the least of which is the magnificent Ardtornish gardens, approximately thirty acres of splendid parkland: shrubs and trees, native birch, larch, firs and pines, dark green against the pink sandstone façade of the great house. Owen and Emmeline Hugh Smith bought the Ardtornish estate in 1930 and each year they received gifts of named and un-named hybrid rhododendrons from Sir John Stirling Maxwell, of Pollock House in Glasgow. Consequently, the Ardtornish plants are famous throughout Scotland for their diversity and vibrant colours.

The gardens at Ardtornish have been developed over a period of 150 years and today they enfold an amazing sense of calm. Well-defined walks lead through this wonderland following the Keeper's Path to a graceful Alpine meadow, Amphitheatre and Eucryphia garden, with a number of "diversions" leading off to further delights. The present incumbents of the estate, the Raven Family, along with local people, have continued to care for the gardens, primarily Faith Raven, who recently published a comprehensive history of the gardens, *The Ardtornish Garden – A Highland Garden in Morvern, Lochaber: History, Gardeners, Seasons and a Tour*. The book is available from the estate office.

Ian Lamb is the present Ardtornish Estate gardener. For twenty-seven years, Ian and his wife, Helen, ran the estate kitchen garden as an independent nursery selling a wide range of both indoor and outdoor plants until, in 2007, they took on the task of helping to care for the main garden. I met Ian on a brisk morning when he was busy pruning the roses that adorn the front of the house. This is no mean task and requires the use of a hydraulic lift to reach the upper areas of the display. Ian lowered his working platform to ground level and came over to speak to me. He is a well-built, bearded man with a ready smile, and the character and stature of one who obviously loves his work. He knows, intimately, every inch of his domain and listening to him talk about the plants and animals that he encounters during his daily tasks was entirely fascinating and inspiring.

Just as fascinating was the time I spent with Simon Boult, the estate head stalker. Simon guides guests on both hill and river and I chatted to him by the old bridge where the River Aline greets the sea in sheltered Loch Aline. Simon had brought along a fishing rod, more in hope than earnest endeavour because the river was running very high. It quickly became apparent to me that he was well versed in its use, casting neatly over the stream whilst avoiding the trees and undergrowth that lined the bank behind him. Simon originally hails from Somerset, in England, but has worked in Scotland for the last twenty-one years, gaining experience in his craft in the Outer Hebrides, Islay, Perthshire, Kintyre and Speyside. As with Ian Lamb, Simon mightily impressed me both with his knowledge and his enthusiasm.

Back at Ardtornish House, Isobel Carmichael, the housekeeper, gave me a guided tour of the building. Isobel, who was born at Ardtornish, has a ready laugh and a wicked sense of humour. The house is huge and if Isobel hadn't been leading the way, I would have very quickly become lost. "Below stairs", where the staff lived, still retains some of the features that must have been in daily use when John Buchan was a guest: a long row of numbered bells, connected to the principal rooms upstairs, set high on the wall and readily visible to the alert eyes and ears of the house staff and butler. What a flurry there must have been when the bells clanged their summons, men and women dashing in all directions to attend to the orders of family and guests.

The entrance hall is magnificent; portraits of family members and Highland scenes adorn the walls and a graceful flight of wide stairs, with a delicately sculptured, shining white banister leading up to the first floor. The great house has been divided into five, private and individual guest suites but Ardtornish still retains a remarkable sense of "wholeness". Magnificent carpets, which have been in place for many years, are preciously guarded and carefully maintained. Each of the suites has similar characteristics: the comfortable sense of a time and way of life that is passing yet, at Ardtornish, is still accessible, fortified with the accoutrements of present-day living.

I asked Isobel what she felt about Ardtornish and she replied instantly, "It is a very special place because it is my home and it is beautiful and I love it." Isobel's father was the estate Foreman and her mother cooked for the Raven Family. I left Isobel with her cheerful team of girls, all busy hoovering, dusting and polishing, preparing the house to receive a flood of eager guests who were to attend a weekend wedding reception at Ardtornish House.

In times past, the estate provided employment for nearly 100 local people. This tradition continues today when fifty to sixty people are recognised as gaining employment from the assets and activities of the estate. The estate was eventually inherited by the Raven Family and it extends to 35,000 acres, occupying the southeast corner of the Morvern peninsula, and, in 1967, the title was transferred into the name of Ardtornish Estate Company Limited. The stated objectives of the company are: To manage the estate, to support the strength and prosperity of the community, to maintain and enhance the natural and cultural heritage, and to develop in a sustainable way the value of the estate for the benefit of both the owners and the community.

This bald statement belies the reality that is Ardtornish. Has the estate succeeded in its aim? The truth is that I don't really know. What I do know, however, is that when I leave the main road and drive down the hill into Ardtornish, it is as though I have passed through an invisible curtain into a different world. A magical land full of "noises and sweet airs that give delight and hurt not". A place where all things are possible and where there is a sense of sublime peace. Go there and discover for yourself the joy that is Ardtornish.

For further details about Ardtornish Estate, accommodation, visitor centre and holiday services, activities, Ardtornish gardens, stalking, shooting and fishing, booking and other information, visit the Ardtornish Estate website at: http:// www.ardtornish.co.uk/; Email: stay@ardtornish.co.uk or contact: Ardtornish Estate Office, Morvern, by Oban, Argyll, Scotland PA80 5UZ; Tel: 01967 421288; Fax: 01967 421221.

32.
Glenelg

If I believed in reincarnation, I would choose, if I could, to come back as an otter. Of all the creatures that grace this magical land I love, *Lutra lutra*, the European otter, is supreme: an outdoor existence, swimming on demand, a highly developed sense of fun and unlimited fishing; all of the things that give me purpose and pleasure in life.

I thought of this as I looked down on Sandaig, a few tortuous, single-track-road miles south from Glenelg in Inverness-shire, with its scattered islands and deserted, shell sand beaches guarding the southern approach to the fierce waters of the Kylerhea narrows. Another otter-lover, Gavin Maxwell, author of *Ring of Bright Water*, lived there in a cottage by the lighthouse on Eilean Mor. His book tells of the otters he befriended at "Camusfearna", the name he gave to Sandaig in his stories.

Visitors make the pilgrimage to "Camusfearna" to pay their respects to Maxwell. He is buried there alongside Edal, his most famous otter, and a huge stone marks the place where his cottage stood. A fire destroyed the cottage in 1968, after which he moved to a cottage by the lighthouse on Eilean Ban – "The White Island" – which now supports one of the piers of the Skye Bridge, built in the 1990s.

Getting to Glenelg, "The Glens of Hunting", is not for the faint-hearted. Loch Alsh and Loch Duich, along the Road to the Isles by gaunt Eilean Donan Castle, bound it to the north. To the south, the dark, cold waters of Loch Hourn separate the Glenelg peninsula from the rough bounds of Knoydart. Westward across the Sound of Sleat is the misty island of Skye and its blue-grey Cuillin hills.

Glenelg, population in the order of 200 souls, is the principal community in this wilderness land, a land dominated by fractured mountains knifed by steep, tortuous passes; Beinn nan Caorach (773m) "Hill of the Rowan Berries", Beinn na h-Eaglaise (804m) "Hill of the Church", Sgurr Mhic Bharraich (781m) "Peak of the Son of Maurice", Beinn Sgritheall (974m) "The Scree Hill". The only other substantial village here is Arnisdale, where the road ends, past Sandaig, a dozen or so miles south along the shores of Loch Hourn.

This road is the only way into this remote peninsula and it follows the line of General Wade's military road built in 1770. Join it at Shiel Bridge at the head of Loch Duich on the A87 road from Invermoriston to Kyle of Lochalsh. The route was constructed in the aftermath of the Jacobite Rebellions and links Fort Augustus at the head of Loch Ness to Bernera Barracks at Glenelg, then the main point of access to the Kylerhea ferry over the sea to Skye.

The road climbs spectacularly from Shiel Bridge across the Bealach Ratagan, giving unforgettable views north to the magnificent peaks of the Five Sisters of Kintail and into the hills and mountains of the Inverinate Forest. Three years after it was completed, two illustrious travellers, Johnson and Boswell, passed this way, as recorded in Boswell's book, *The Journal of a Tour to the Hebrides with Samuel Johnson, LL.D.*

Of the road over the bealach, Dr Johnson commented: "We left Auknasheals and the Macraes in the afternoon and in the evening came to Ratiken, a high hill upon which a road is cut, but so steep and narrow that it is very difficult. Upon one of the precipices, my horse, weary with the steepness of the rise, staggered a little, and I called in haste to the Highlander to hold him. This was the only moment of my journey in which I thought myself endangered."

Even today, drivers treat this road with respect but once the bealach is surmounted, the vista that unfolds is remarkable. It is as though the traveller has discovered an entirely unexpected, secret world: a sudden, fertile strath, graced by a tumbling stream, busy with fine black-faced sheep, cattle and croft cottages; bounded on either side by majestic peaks and, ahead, the splendid mountains of Skye. The road twists and turns down to Glenelg village, clustered comfortably about a sheltered bay facing the blue waters of the Sound of Sleat.

Johnson and Boswell stopped at the old Ferry Inn, by the Kylerhea narrows, and the following morning crossed over to Skye where they met Flora MacDonald and her husband at Kingsburgh. Johnson famously said of the lady, "Her name will be mentioned in history and if courage and fidelity be virtues, mentioned with honour."

After the 1715 Jacobite uprising, the sea-crossing was deemed to be so important to the security of the country that government ordered the building of the military barracks at Bernera to protect it. A ferry, the *Glenachulish*, the last working example of a turntable-ferry in Scotland, still plies the Kylerhea narrows during the summer months and is owned and run by the Isle of Skye Ferry Community Interest Company.

Two less-illustrious travellers, your correspondent and a friend, made the journey last November. We caught the last rays of the winter sun as we arrived at the top of Bealach Ratagan and were, like so many others, captivated by the majesty of the view that lay before us. However, by the time we arrived in Glenelg, darkness enfolded us, but the light was on in our cottage and our host was there to greet us.

Sunset in these airts during winter months comes at about 3.30pm, so, after unpacking, we went up to the village where we found the community hall busy with residents enjoying afternoon tea and home-made scones to die for. Within moments, we were chatting happily to local people, sharing our thoughts on Glenelg and learning a little of what makes it such a friendly and welcoming place. A gaggle of laughing boys and girls joined us, freed from school, soon to be hurried off homewards to waiting parents.

As is often the case in Highland communities, the population is astonishingly cosmopolitan – a mix of people who were born and bred in Glenelg and had lived there all their lives, and others who had left to find employment in the south and then returned to the place they so clearly loved; and, of course, refugees from the mad, satanic mills of Glasgow and

Edinburgh and the Central Belt, and even from further afield. Indeed, the woman serving tea, a happy, bright, smiling, vibrant presence, was from São Paulo in Brazil.

I fell into conversation with one such refugee, Edwin Stiven, playwright, scriptwriter, tutor and occasional actor. Eddie originally hails from Ayrshire and is gloriously bearded and articulate. I asked what had brought him to Glenelg and he told me, "It is just a wonderful and inspiring place for a writer, peaceful and quiet." Eddie is a member of the Scottish Society of Playwrights and of the actors union, Equity. His work has appeared at the Edinburgh Festival Fringe and the Traverse Theatre and at the Tron Theatre in Glasgow. When I spoke with him in 2010, he was working on a commission for BBC Radio Scotland for his play *Wings of the Morning* (see: www.eddiestiven.co.uk).

The following morning, I headed for the village shop, indeed just about the only shop in Glenelg, for bread and a newspaper. There we met the owners, two more refugees from the suburbs of Glasgow, Jane and Craig Scobie. I asked Jane if she missed the bustle and hustle of the "Dear Green Place". Without hesitation, she replied, "We have been here for four years now and would never go back. Living here is like the difference between living in heaven and hell." The shop was full of laughter, reflecting the character of the proprietors.

I met another group of characters in the afternoon, the members of the Glenelg fire service. They had agreed to be photographed during a practice meeting and gathered, laughing and joking, round their fire engine for the event. They were a supremely happy team but it was immediately obvious that they were also highly disciplined and capable in their role. The vast area they have to cover and the difficult roads they have to traverse in order to reach outlying communities is awesome, but they carry out their vital work with the utmost professionalism.

One of the most surprising sights in Glenelg is the War Memorial. It stands in a clear space by the shores of the Sound of Sleat and is magnificent: a startling group of bronze figures set on a tall plinth. It was created by the sculptor and artist Louis Reid Deuchars (1870–1927), and planned over two years in collaboration with the famous Scottish architect Sir Robert Lorimer (1864–1929). The statue shows an angel holding aloft a laurel wreath, reaching down to help a kneeling woman. They are flanked on the left by the figure of a soldier, a Cameron Highlander, standing at ease with his rifle and steel helmet.

The memorial was commissioned by Lady Scott of Eilanreach to commemorate her son, George, and her son-in-law, Roland Hebeler, and the twenty others from the community who were killed during the First World War. The first name on the memorial is Major Valentine Fleming DSO, the father of Ian Fleming, the writer and creator of "James Bond". The family owned the Arnisdale Estate. Winston Churchill wrote an obituary for Major Valentine that Ian Fleming framed and kept by him all his life.

There are memorials to an older people who lived and worked here more than 2,000 years ago: the dramatic remains of their brochs in Glen Beag, to the south of Glenelg. The brochs were circular, dry-stone-built towers, enclosing a space of 40yds and approximately 12m in height. Dun Telve Broch is one of the best preserved of these structures in Europe. Nearby, on the side of the hill to the left of the road, are the remains of another broch, Dun Troddan, which, if anything, is perhaps more dramatic than Telve. I climbed the hill and mounted the wall enclosing the inner courtyard. From this vantage point, I looked out over the same landscape that these ancient people must have surveyed and felt their presence by me.

The presence of Alice Macalonan was just as impressive. Alice was born and brought up in Glenelg and had agreed to meet me. She is a charming lady, with kindly eyes and a smile that mightily brightened the grey, winter's day when we sat chatting before the fire in her comfortable living room. Like many of her peers, Alice had to leave Glenelg to find employment and worked for many years with children at Yorkhill hospital in Glasgow.

Her parents had the village post office and shop, and during the Second World War, they managed the local telephone exchange. Her mother used to get up at 4am and, after milking the cows, would "man" the phone so that her husband could have a rest. Life was simple when Alice was a girl, entertainment homemade, playing chess, draughts, whist and a lot of knitting. Electricity didn't arrive in Glenelg until 1950 and coal was brought in by sea.

Her mother used to say that the best part of her days was the early morning, in the spring of the year, in the fields, listening to the cry of green plover, the constant tide washing the shore, the silence and the smell of peat smoke and of the sea. "I just love Glenelg," Alice told me. "Its roots are so deep in me that I know that I could not be happy anywhere else."

When I left Glenelg, I paused on Bealach Ratagan and looked back. The village by the shore glinted silver and gold in winter sunlight. Smoke drifted lazily from the croft cottages that lay scattered up and down the glen. A dog barked somewhere and a hunting buzzard circled above the white thread of a tumbling stream where otters still play. It was hard to leave such peace and certainty, hard to turn our backs on such magical beauty.

33.

John O'Groats to Durness Drive
Part One:
John O'Groats to Forss House Hotel

Come with me this morning on a magical journey through time and history, along the furthermost reaches of mainland Scotland's north coast; by croft and castle and red-scarred cliffs loud with the cry of wheeling gulls, where white-fingered green waves endlessly caress near-deserted yellow sand beaches, distant blue mountains beckon and golden eagles soar.

To get the best out of this drive, you need three UK maps: Ordnance Survey Map 12, Thurso, Wick and surrounding area; Map 10, Strathnaver; and Map 9, Cape Wrath – all in the Landranger series, Scale 1:50,000. View these maps at http://getamap.ordnancesurvey.co.uk or buy paper copies direct from the Ordnance Shop on the same site. Be well prepared.

We begin in the east, at Duncansby Head, near John O'Groats, and travel west from there along the A836 through Thurso to Tongue, and thence follow the A838 round sea loch Eriboll to journey's end in the tiny village of Durness, a total distance of 100 miles. Along the way, we will pass through the ancient heartlands of clans Sinclair, Gunn, Sutherland and Mackay, who for centuries filled the straths with the bellowing belligerence of their constant feuds.

How long the journey takes is entirely up to you but you should plan for at least one overnight stop. A week is much better, because there is so much to see and do and explore amidst this amazing landscape. You may be as active or as passive as you wish, but my advice would be to pack at least stout walking boots and wet weather gear; in Caithness, the walking is easy, however, out in the wilds of Sutherland, leaving the car and striking off into the wilderness can be much more vigorous entertainment.

Ann and I have lived in these airts for nearly forty years, firstly in Caithness and, for the past twenty years, in a cottage overlooking the Kyle of Tongue, out beyond the "split stane", the old boundary stone dividing Caithness from Sutherland. We know and love the area dearly, and have tramped and hiked over most of it, under the cathedral-like skies of the wonderful Flow Country moorlands of Caithness to the jagged peaks of Ben Loyal, the Queen of Scottish mountains. We find comfort and pleasure in every season the Good Lord sends us and there is no other place on Planet Earth where we would rather live.

In truth, John O'Groats can be a disappointment, although there are plans to brush up its image. It is, nevertheless, a landmark Scottish destination and, as such, it is a must-see port-of-call for most visitors. However, if you follow the little road east from John O'Groats to Duncansby Head and park by the white-painted lighthouse, you will begin to appreciate the real worth of Caithness. The view from the lighthouse is reason enough for making this detour: a distant prospect over the deserted island of Stroma to the Orkney Isles and, even nicer, if you walk south along the cliff path, the jagged Stacks of Duncansby; sea-girt sandstone pillars, the tallest of which, the Great Stack, is 61m in height. During the nesting season, the cliffs are crowded with squabbling birds, including stiff-winged fulmar, guillemot, black wing-tipped kittiwake and firework-beaked puffins.

Driving west from John O'Groats, the island of Stroma dominates the northern view. Stroma was inhabited for hundreds of years and the population was essentially self-sufficient, growing most of their own food. In the first *Scottish Statistical Account*, published in 1793, the minister of Canisbay Church, the Rev. John Morrison, describes the people of Stroma thus: "From their political situation, and the simplicity, sobriety and industry, natural to them, there are perhaps few islanders on earth happier than those of Stroma." Stroma was once home to nearly 400 people but by 1962, the island was deserted as the population left to seek greater opportunities on the mainland. You may visit Stroma by charter boat from John O'Groats.

At Kirkstyle, two miles west from John O'Groats, call and make your peace with your maker at lovely Canisbay Church. The late Queen Mother often worshiped there when staying in her northern home at the Castle of Mey. The original structure probably dates back to the fifteenth century, although there is mention of a church here in 1222. The pre-reformation tower in the centre of the west front is an echo of the enormous changes that were reshaping religious attitudes throughout Europe at that time. By 1581, Caithness had been divided into presbyteries, however, after the restoration of King Charles II in 1660, the old Episcopalian faith flourished again in the county.

Throughout our journey, the sea will be our constant companion, from the ever-turbulent waters of the uproarious Pentland Firth, to the wide reaches of the Atlantic Ocean. Bewhiskered seals abound, curiously marking your passage. Porpoise, dolphin and orcas are often seen, particularly in the Pentland Firth, and sightings of great minkie whales are not uncommon. At Gills Bay, where the ultra-modern catamaran *Pentalina* operates a car and passenger service to St Margaret's Hope in Orkney, the road runs close to the shore. I have never passed this way without seeing seals resting and preening themselves on the rocks below the road. Stop and make their acquaintance.

An excellent place for lunch is in the new restaurant adjacent to the Castle of Mey. The castle and gardens are open to visitors from April through to September and offer the opportunity to explore the late Queen Mother's home, which she bought following the death of her husband in 1952. It is very much as she left it, with her favourite personal belongings on display – books, pictures and memorabilia of her lasting fondness of Caithness and the surrounding lands.

A few minutes further west brings you to Loch St John's, one of Scotland's most famous wild brown trout lochs where, if you are so inclined, fishing is readily available to visiting anglers. St John's is also famous for its ability to cure physical and mental ailments. Those who suffered would walk or be carried round the shores of the loch, bathe in its waters, throw a silver coin into the loch and depart without looking back. In Dunnet village, look forward to a visit to Mary-Ann Calder's croft house, built more than 150 years ago and in which Mary-Ann lived for nearly ninety years. The cottage is now owned by the Caithness Heritage Trust and remarkably reflects the way in which crofters lived and worked during the nineteenth century and early years of the twentieth century.

A minor road points north from Dunnet, leading you through the scattered township of Brough to the lighthouse on the cliffs at Dunnet Head, the most northerly point on mainland Scotland. The lighthouse stands 91m above the silver-leaden sea and the structure is 20m in height. Robert Stevenson, grandfather of the wonderful Scottish author and poet Robert Louis Stevenson, built it in 1831. Dunnet Head marks the westerly entrance to the tortuous waters of the Pentland Firth – the eastern limit is Duncansby Head. In the days of sail, pilots were ferried out to waiting ships to safely conduct them through these dangerous seas.

There are a series of little lochs on Dunnet Head, the largest being the Long Loch, which was traditionally used for racing model yachts. Another of the Dunnet Head lochs, Loch of Bushta, in the southwest quarter of the peninsula was, when we lived in Caithness, my private swimming pool. On hot summer days, I would walk out past the tiny beach below the statuesque House of the Northern Gate, and along the edge of the jagged cliffs over Dwarick Head to reach the loch. The water is crystal clear and the south end has a soft, sandy bottom, making it ideal for an invigorating splash. When I arrived at the loch, I was invariably greeted by a curious red-throated diver who would flap off crossly the moment I invaded his privacy. Dunnet Head really requires a whole day to properly appreciate all that it has to offer. It is, in its own right, a wildlife paradise, rich in flora and fauna, and a circuit of the whole headland is one of the great walks of Caithness.

Nearby Dunnet Bay has one of Scotland's most stunning beaches, two miles of spotless, golden sands. The beach is considered to be "crowded" if you can see a few other people in the distance. This was one of our favourite family walks at Christmas and New Year, the whole of Clan Sandison, complete with friends and relations and dogs various, marching together companionably along the shore. Visiting snow buntings, flocks of fluttering flakes, whisked by. Seals sometimes followed our progress with sad-eyed caution and, on one occasion, we were blessed with the company of a great northern diver, majestically afloat beyond the surf.

Castletown, our next stop, has many claims to fame, not the least of which is being the birthplace of the ancestors of one of America's most iconic heroes, General George Armstrong Custer, he of Little Bighorn fame. But Castletown is best known as being the birthplace of the Caithness Flagstone industry, which blossomed under the tutelage of James Traill of Rattar (1758–1843), Sheriff of Caithness. Nearly 400 million years ago, the whole of the north of Scotland, well out into what is now the North Sea, was covered by what is known as the Sea of Orcadies. As the sea dried, successive layers of sediment were laid down and this was the source of the flagstone for which Caithness became renowned during the nineteenth century and for which it is still renowned to this day; the beauty of the flagstone lies in the simplicity with which it can be split and dressed, often by hand, without the need for mechanical intervention. The stone has been used for hundreds of years by Caithness people, as fencing in a largely treeless landscape and for house building, roofing tiles and walls.

The industry thrived in an age when railways were being developed throughout Britain. Many of the platforms required to service the puffing steam-driven monsters were paved with Caithness flagstone. The Strand in London was paved with the material, as was the concourse of Euston Station and Waverley Station in Edinburgh. At its height in 1902, the industry produced 35,363 tonnes of flagstone valued £23,239 and Caithness flagstone was being sent all over the world, including to Australia and South America. Much of the stone was exported from Castletown Harbour and the harbour has been finely renovated using this most enduring of all building stones. Find out more about the industry by following the Castlehill Flagstone Trail in Castletown, a substantial community initiative that will lead you through the story of the stone with past sculptures formed from it by local artists.

Fifteen minutes further west brings us to the Royal Burgh of Thurso, clustered around a bay at the mouth of the Thurso River, one of Scotland's most notable salmon streams, where anglers catch upwards of 900 wild salmon each year. Thurso is a welcoming place that has expanded mightily since the building of the UK's first nuclear power station at Dounreay, a few miles to the west of the town, in the 1950s. However, Thurso has a long history of occupation, through Neolithic times and the days of Viking domination of the far north, to the battles and struggles of the Middle Ages when the Kingdom of Scotland was being forged. Members of the Sinclair family are the pre-eminent Lairds here and their leaders have always played an important role in the great affairs of state throughout the ages.

Sir John Sinclair (1754–1835), born in Thurso Castle, is perhaps most famously remembered for introducing cheviot sheep to Caithness and Sutherland, an introduction that subsequently led to the tragedy of the great clearances of the nineteenth century. Sir John was President of the Board of Agriculture and he was responsible for the publication of the remarkable first *Statistical Account of Scotland (1791–1799)*, a detailed description of every parish in Scotland written primarily by their local ministers. The present Laird, John Sinclair, Lord Thurso, represents the county in the UK's Westminster Parliament.

Thurso is our principal shopping centre, an hour's drive from where we live in Tongue, and we visit it generally twice a month to restock the Sandison larder. The journey is never irksome, always exciting and full of interest along the way. However, my favourite part of Thurso is somewhat less modern than the local supermarkets. It is the ruins of St Peter's Church, near to the harbour and in the oldest part of the town. There has probably been a church on this site since the thirteenth century, although the present structure dates primarily from the sixteenth and seventeenth centuries. There is a beautiful stone-latticed window and St Peter's has, to me, an air of serenity that is almost touchable, a corner of calm amidst the storm of living.

Another corner of serenity, for an entirely different reason, may be found at Scrabster Harbour: the Captain's Galley (Tel: 01847 894999), adjudged in 2009 to be the UK's "Best Seafood Restaurant". After such a busy day, you deserve nothing but the best. And for complete rest and relaxation, drive west from Thurso for ten minutes to spend the night at Forss House Hotel (Tel: 01847 861201), a gracious building on the banks of a small river set amidst ancient woodlands, close to Crosskirk Bay and the endless chorus of the sea.

34.
John O'Groats to Durness Drive
Part Two:
Forss House Hotel to Durness

Forss House Hotel stands on a green space overlooking a gracious salmon stream. To the left of the house, by the side of the lawn, a path leads to a promontory overlooking a dramatic waterfall, ever more dramatic after heavy rain. A thoughtfully placed seat overlooks the falls and the dark pool below. Early one morning, as I sat there, I watched an otter slide confidently into the pool. His whiskers twitched as he scented the air for the hint of any unwanted presence. I watched him pursue, capture and bustle ashore a large salmon, rushing the doomed fish into the undergrowth, anxious for breakfast.

A track at the back of the house, through an iron gate, takes you along pine-wooded hills above the river, where, below, the Forss glides gently seawards through green meadowlands adorned with spotted orchid, marsh marigold, buttercup, violet, forget-me-not, comfrey and speedwell, milkwort and primrose. In warm corners *Primula scotica*, one of the rarest and most unique of all Scottish plants, blushes purple-pink in spring sunlight. Black and white wagtails dip and bob by the stream as it hurries under a footbridge to greet the cold Atlantic in Crosskirk Bay. On the cliffs above the west shore, visit the ruins of one of the oldest places of worship in the north, the twelfth century St Mary's Chapel. Tread softly amongst the grey stones and listen to the whisper of the passing winds of time.

Reluctantly leaving Forss House, we now head west and continue our journey into the depths of Sutherland and the Land of Clan Mackay, past the ominous form of Dounreay Atomic Power Station, now being decommissioned, and the ever-expanding village of Reay. Those inflicted with the pain of golf should consider a round at Reay, a traditional and very attractive 18-hole links course established in 1893. No need to book a tee time, £25 per round, excellent value for money and famous for the friendly welcome visitors receive. A few miles further west from Reay, on the right-hand side of the road, stands the "Split Stane"; a huge boulder that, according to legend, the Devil, angry with delays on his journey west, cleaved with a mighty blow of his tail.

The "Split Stane" also marks the traditional boundary between Caithness and Sutherland. It was here, during the terrible years of the nineteenth-century Sutherland Clearances, that the people of Caithness gathered to greet these destitute families and offer them comfort and assistance. It was not always thus, for Clan Mackay were once one of the most powerful clans in the north, famous for their constant feuding, both with their neighbours and amongst themselves. Their most persistent foes were Clan Sutherland, with whom they were forever at odds. However, that which the Sutherlands could not obtain by force of arms, they eventually achieved, in 1829, through purchase. In that year, the last of the Clan Mackay lands were acquired by the Earl of Sutherland from his financially distraught neighbour. The "Bratach Bhan", the white banner of the ancient clan, fluttered no more.

A series of long, lonely river straths, running north to south, divides these northlands. The first, Strath Halladale, where the River Halladale empties into the sea through the golden sands fringing Melvich Bay, gives visitors their initial glimpse of the remarkable beaches and bays that lie ahead, each one demanding further inspection. Strath Halladale itself offers much to delight both eye and mind, not the least of which is the Royal Society for the Protection of Birds (RSPB) Flow Country nature reserve. The Flow Country of Caithness and Sutherland is one of the last remaining and most important examples of blanket bog peatlands on Planet Earth. My family and I have spent many, many happy days walking in the Flow country; fishing its sparkling silver and blue lochs for wild brown trout; meeting fearsome, scowling wild cats, playful families of otters, statuesque red deer, soaring golden eagle and hunting hen harriers. Visit the RSPB centre at Forsinard and join one of their guided walks to discover the full glory of this entirely magical wonderland.

A fine new road hurries the traveller west now, across the moor to the tiny township of Strathy, which has its own, yellow gem of a beach. Turn right in Strathy and follow the narrow, twisting road out to Totegan to visit Strathy Point, where a lighthouse casts its welcoming beam to mariners for a distance of up to twenty-six miles. Strathy is also remarkable for the fact that it has no less than four churches, built between 1829 and 1910. The first of the churches was designed and built by Thomas Telford (1757–1834), a towering genius who made an enormous impact on the far north: piers, harbours, canals, towns – such as Ullapool in Wester Ross and Pulteneytown in Wick, Caithness. His Strathy church was funded by the government, in one of the first acts of "public relations", to try to persuade highlanders that those in far off London really cared for both their physical and moral welfare. When the church was completed, the government also paid the minister's stipend, the princely sum of £120 per annum.

At the start of our journey to Durness and Cape Wrath, back in Caithness at John O'Groats, I suggested that those following this trail should consider taking at least a week to complete the route. Perhaps now is a good time to remind you of this suggestion. There really is so much to see and do, so many places to visit and explore, that it would be sad to miss them. As such, as we come to the heart of the Mackay Country, around the small communities of Bettyhill and Tongue, it is useful to note that there is a wide range of accommodation here to suit everyone: excellent hotels, guest houses, B&B establishments and camping sites. Find out which is for you by visiting www.scotland-inverness.co.uk/caithness.htm. Spend a few days exploring the surrounding countryside, enjoying the beaches, hills and mountains that make this area one of the jewels in Scotland's crown.

Bettyhill, which we reach after a half hour's drive from Strathy, is forever linked to the infamous Sutherland Clearances. Many think that the name, "Bettyhill" is inherited from Elizabeth, Countess Duchess of Sutherland, whose husband, George Leveson-Gower, 1st Duke of Sutherland, was a prime architect of this atrocious act. But there are indications that the little township clinging to broken cliffs at the mouth of the River Naver had been known as Bettyhill for many years prior to the clearances: an old woman called Betty lived in a house on a hill there and gave her name to the community.

Whatever the truth of the origin of the name, it is forever emotive of all the hardship the Sutherland family visited upon their defenceless dependents. The full story is told in the old church by Farr Beach, now the Strathnaver Museum, on your right just before you enter the village. In 1819, the Rev. David Mackenzie read the eviction notices from the pulpit. Not so very long ago, I stood in that same pulpit, recording a programme for BBC Radio Scotland, and read out paragraphs of what the minister had said. It brought tears to my eyes then and still does to this day when I think about how helpless and hopeless those who heard the words must have felt.

For me, the River Naver, which flows down from the heights of Ben Klibreck and Ben Hee, will always be the "river of a thousand tears". But it is hard to be sad for long in Bettyhill today. This is a thriving, bustling community with a vibrant secondary school that offers local children all that is best in education; and I speak from personal experience, given that three of my grandchildren are pupils there. And the history of Strathnaver records remarkable evidence of human habitation reaching back to Mesolithic times, 10,000 years ago, when the first hunter gatherers settled on the shores of Torrisdale Bay, where the river tumbles into the sea.

On the raised beach on the west bank of the Naver, buried under centuries of sand, are the remains of more than a dozen hut circles built and inhabited 5,000 years ago during the Neolithic period. Ruined brochs, circular stone-built towers of up to 12m in height, zig-zag south on either side of the river for a distance of nearly twenty miles, built during the period 200 BC to AD 200. There are relics from the days of Viking dominance, from the ninth century, and the outlines of traditional turf-roofed long-houses from the Middle Ages; and there are scattered boulders of the homes of those who were evicted. For full details on all the above and details of the Strathnaver Trail, which takes you to these sites, see: www.strathnavermuseum. org.uk.

I have to confess a vested interest in the village of Tongue, our next stopping place on the way west: I have lived there for almost twenty years and many members of my family have also made their homes in the vicinity. We live in a small croft cottage looking directly onto the jagged ridge of Ben Loyal, the Queen of Scottish mountains. To the west towers Ben Hope, Scotland's most northerly Munro, whilst from our back door we survey the wide, shallow Kyle of Tongue, dominated on a hill overlooking the village by the ruins of Castle Varrich, a fifteenth-century Clan Mackay fortress, which probably also served as a Viking stronghold in earlier times. On warm summer evenings, the scent of peat smoke spreads from the chimneys of village houses and, in winter, the black night sky twinkles with myriad stars and, often, the breathtaking sparkle of the Northern Lights.

As is the case with most of these far-flung lands, signs of man's activity abound. Close to the east shore of Loch Hakel, a few minutes' drive from the centre of the village, there is a vast boulder on the surface of which are inscribed the most significant assembly of cup-and-ring markings to be found anywhere in Europe, cut there some 5,000 years ago by people who lived by the loch. There are the remains of a ruined Pictish fort on a tiny island nearby and, on a ridge to the south east of the loch, at Drum nan Coup, the site of the last battle fought in Sutherland between Clan Sutherland and Clan Mackay; reported to have been a bloody, broadsword and battleaxe affair that the Mackays famously won. Loch Hakel is also reputed to be where, in 1746, survivors of the French vessel *Hazzard*, pursued and attacked by British warships in the Kyle of Tongue, flung into the loch handfuls of gold coins destined for the embattled Highland army of Bonnie Prince Charlie at Culloden.

There are wonderful walks along the wide, near-deserted sands at Torrisdale, by the scattered township of Skerray, and the chance, on calm days, of sailing to deserted Island Roan, "The Island of Seals", a mile off-shore from Skerray Harbour. The island was once the home to a self-sufficient community of nearly 100 people. Enjoy lazy, sunny picnics on warm beaches at the Rabbit Islands, guarding the mouth of Kyle. The Kyle itself is popular with windsurfers and small-boat sailors, as it is with anglers fishing for the sea-bass and sea-trout that enter on successive tides. From our cottage windows, we often see golden eagle, buzzard, raven and peregrine falcons going about their daily affairs, and on one memorable occasion, sea eagles, attacking sea gulls, sheltering in our glen from the full force of a mighty storm. You will always find a warm welcome in Tongue and friendly people always willing to help.

We are now nearing the end of our journey, crossing the narrow ribbon of the causeway that bridges the Kyle of Tongue, speeding over the desolate moorlands of the Moine Peninsula towards the River Hope and Loch Hope. The horizon is lined by majestic mountains: Ben Hope itself in the foreground, backed by the Reay Forest peaks of Arkle, Foinaven, Cranstackie and Beinn Spionnaidh, and in the far distance, the hills of Cape Wrath.

Our way winds round Loch Eriboll, the deepest sea-loch in the north of Scotland, from where *HMS Hood* sailed into the Atlantic to confront and face disaster from the guns of the German battleship *Bismarck*. On a hill to the west, overlooking the loch, stones, painted white and formed into the names of the ships that anchored there, are set out near the summit.

A remarkable change in the landscape occurs as you leave Loch Eriboll and turn west on the final run to the village of Durness. Where, before, wild heather and sphagnum-clad moors crowded the way, the land changes to verdant, green pastures. This change has been caused by a limestone outcrop, born many miles to the south in the islands of the Inner Hebrides, which surfaces again before dipping once more below the cold waters of the Atlantic Ocean.

This gives Durness and the surrounding area a special character and provides a wonderful habitat for a wide variety of flora and fauna. The crystal-clear lochs here offer some of the finest trout fishing in the world. During the early months of the year, the sea-girt cliffs are home to thousands of nesting birds. Shore-side, cathedral-like caves invite easy exploration. Stay in Durness for a few days and enjoy the peace and content that it enfolds.

Whilst doing so, prepare for one final, exciting expedition by sea, mini-bus and foot to the lighthouse on the north-west tip of the Cape Wrath peninsula, to marvel at the stark, vast, 160-metre-high cliffs, constantly washed by 3,000-mile-old, green Atlantic waves, and, surprisingly, for a coffee in the most remote café in Scotland. John Ure and his wife Kay bought and renovated one of the disused lighthouse keeper's cottages and opened it as a café. Have a look at www.durness.org for all the details of visits to Cape Wrath and for full information on all that Durness has to offer.

Thank you for joining me on this journey. We have travelled a long way together and, yet, I feel that there is so much that I have left unsaid, and so much more to what I have said. However, I hope that you have enjoyed the trip, and that you might be tempted to head north and discover it in reality. When you do, you will not be disappointed.

35.
The Royal and Ancient Burgh of Wick

Hidden within our souls is a deep-rooted love of the land that gave us birth. Those of us who were born in Scotland and those who have Scottish ancestors celebrated this truth during 2009, the Year of the Scottish Homecoming. I began my journey home in 1976, after many years living in the north east of England. Circumstances meant that we could choose any place on Planet Earth in which to live. My wife, Ann, and I talked it over with our four children; well, to be precise, three of them – the fourth, little Jean, was only six months old then. We agreed that we should move to Caithness, where my paternal grandfather had been born in the tiny fishing village of Staxigoe, close to the Royal Burgh of Wick.

My father spent many of his childhood holidays staying with an uncle, George Rae, who farmed near Wick. He told me that when Granddad was a young man, he and a group of friends were walking across the old bridge that arches the River Wick in the centre of town. On the opposite side of the bridge, a group of pretty girls were hurrying by, talking and laughing as only a group of pretty girls can do. Granddad and his friends were watching them, as young men do, and one said to him, "You see that girl over there, the brown-haired lassie in the middle? I bet you wouldn't dare go across and kiss her." My granddad didn't hesitate. He crossed the road and kissed her, and two years later they were married.

I have a formal picture of them on the wall above my desk, monochrome and fading, taken in later life. They are in their Sunday best, sitting at a table graced by a vase of spring flowers. They are smiling, grandmother in a simple dark dress with a single strand of pearls at her throat, grandfather sporting a neatly trimmed moustache, in a suit, wing-collared shirt and tie, with the chain of a pocket watch glimpsed across his waistcoat. Grandma was a Macgregor from Amulree in Perthshire and she and her family were travelling people, coming north each summer to Caithness to sell the goods that they had made during the winter months.

Wick is still a busy, bustling town and offers a wide range of activities throughout the year that are guaranteed to keep everybody happy and occupied, local and visitor alike: a vibrant Gala Week with fun events every day and concluding with a splendid bonfire and fireworks display by the banks of the Wick River; a Continental Market in the town square featuring food and flowers and other produce from a dozen countries; the annual Music Festival, in the town's Assembly rooms, with performers of all ages from all aspects of Wick society; theatre and dance, art exhibitions in the library's St Fergus Gallery, ceilidhs and concerts, lectures and slideshows.

Wick is the administrative centre and the county town of Caithness, often known as the "Lowlands beyond the Highlands" because, unlike neighbouring Sutherland, Caithness is low lying with only a few mountains in the south. The town is backed by fertile farmlands and clusters round the shallow, rock-strewn waters of Wick Bay, which has been an important harbour and trading port almost since history began. The name Wick is derived from the Norse word "Vik" meaning "bay" and for many years Caithnesians lived under Viking rule. That rule ended in September 1263, when the young King Alexander III of Scotland defeated the forces of King Hakon IV of Norway in the Battle of Largs.

The man who led the king's soldiers into that battle was Sir William Sinclair and as a reward, he was granted the lands of Rosslyn near Edinburgh and most of what is present-day Caithness. In spite of being so distant from the centre of power, Clan Sinclair has always played an important part in the events that shaped Scotland. From their arrival from France with William the Conqueror, the Sinclairs served Scotland: they fought with William Wallace at the Battle of Stirling Bridge in 1297, with Robert the Bruce at Bannockburn in 1314, and died with King James IV on Flodden Field in 1513.

Caithness is a land of cliffs and castles, twenty-five in all, and one of the best preserved of these lies close to Wick: Sinclair and Girnigoe Castles, one of the most dramatic ruins in the north of Scotland and built towards the end of the fifteenth century by William, the 2nd Earl of Caithness. The twin castles crown the crest of a narrow, finger-like promontory four miles to the north of town, near Noss Head Lighthouse. They are easily accessible and have recently undergone substantial repairs to preserve them and make them as safe as possible for visitors. Just as dramatic is the Castle of Old Wick, on the southern skirts of the town. It probably dates back to Viking times and was certainly an important castle when Robert the Bruce restored Scottish independence. It is now a roofless tower but still three stories in height with two-metre-thick walls, overlooking the sea and guarded on two sides by twenty-four-metre-high, sheer cliffs.

The old, grey town of Wick, with its narrow streets and sombre buildings, seems to ring with echoes of its turbulent past. The principal street – indeed, the only street for quite a few centuries – is High Street, running from the Parish Church in the west, down to the harbour in the east; still known to this day as "the camps" because Oliver Cromwell's soldiers were billeted there during the seventeenth century when they visited Wick to suppress any unseemly mirth and jollity in the Lord Protector's austere Commonwealth. The officers in Cromwell's army were more appropriately accommodated in Ackergill Tower, a fifteenth-century tower, restored and renovated in the 1980s, complete with the UK's most northerly opera house, and now run as an internationally renowned corporate business venue.

Wick was granted the status of Royal Burgh in 1589 by King James VI, giving the elected councillors powers to hold markets, deal in all manner of goods and other transactions and to levy taxes to be used in the furtherance of the common good of all the people of the Burgh. They did so to excellent effect, particularly in the nineteenth century, during the silver years of the great herring fishings. During the short summer fishing season, more than 1,000 boats crowded the harbour and upwards of 5,000 Gaelic-speaking people from throughout the Highlands flocked to Wick to crew the boats and to clean, pack and sell the fish caught. However, Wick, like Kirkwall in Orkney and Lerwick in Shetland, has always been more Norse than Gaelic and the Gaelic language was rarely heard outwith the fishing season.

The sea is a constant facet of life in Wick, ever present and ever changing, from the mirror stillness of the bay on a warm summer day to the outrageous temper of huge winter storms. Evidence of these days is wonderfully displayed at the Wick Heritage Centre, an award-winning museum near the harbour in Bank Row that was born out of the dedicated efforts of a few local people determined to honour and preserve the history of their community. One of the exhibits is the original light from Noss Head Lighthouse. Like the word "wick", the word "noss" is also derived from Old Norse and means "nose". The lighthouse was designed by Alan Stevenson, one of the members of the famous family of engineers who built so many lighthouses round the coast of Scotland, and it was completed in 1849.

One of the oldest traditions associated with Wick and the herring fishings was the annual appointment of the Wick herring queen. The herring queen reigned for three days and opened her reign by sailing into Wick harbour on the bow of a finely decked-out fishing boat at the head of a flotilla of other fishing boats. The ceremony was last performed more than fifty years ago and has been revived to coincide with the Wick Harbourfest, a special homecoming event that has attracted not only regional, but also national and international recognition. After being crowned, the queen and her court travels in procession around the Pulteneytown area of Wick, built in the nineteenth century to accommodate the expansion of the herring fishing industry. On the Sunday, the herring queen conducts a farewell ceremony before the flotilla sails away and a "Hymns of the Sea" church service is held in the evening.

Often, on visits south, when I had to attend to business in London, Edinburgh or Glasgow, the people I met asked where I lived: "Wick" I would reply. "Really?" would come the astonished response. It was difficult for them to appreciate everything that remote communities such as Wick have to offer: a close-knit society where children can play safely and where serious crime is essentially absent; schools that are amongst the finest in the kingdom. Our children thrived mightily and we never regretted our decision to come home to Wick.

It is only fair to confess, however, that Ann and I did have a vested interest in making that decision: we both love the great outdoors. In that regard, Wick not only provided a comprehensive array of urban facilities, but also wonderful access to the wilds: the amazing beauty of the Caithness moorlands and its unique flora and fauna; superb salmon, sea-trout and wild brown trout fishing; stunning golf courses; glorious, near-empty beaches; cathedral-like skies and the endless peace of the long, endless summer days of the "simmer dim".

One of our first outings after we settled in Wick was a visit to Staxigoe to see where Grandfather had been born. We found a sheltered, boat-bobbing harbour, guarded by a pillar of rock, backed by a few houses and the ruined outlines of the fishermen's cottages where he and his parents once lived. We had taken along a picnic and a bottle of champagne. On the quayside in afternoon sunlight, amidst the music of white-tipped waves gently rocking the little pebbles on the shore, I proposed that famous old Scottish toast, "to absent friends".

36.
Her Majesty The Queen Mother and the Castle of Mey

On a warm autumn afternoon last year, I stood in the sunlit library of the Castle of Mey, the Caithness home of Her Majesty The Queen Mother. In her later years, the Queen Mother used the library as her private sitting room. It remains today much as it must have been when she was there, surrounded by her most favourite books, alongside treasured personal gifts and precious family photographs.

I was not surprised to see volumes on the shelves about Aberdeen Angus cattle and North Country Cheviot sheep, native breeds that the Queen Mother introduced to her nearby farm at Longoe, as well as books on the country sports that she enjoyed all her life. For many years, the Queen Mother's holiday reading list was published in the national press and one of my proudest moments came when I found that one of my books, *The Sporting Gentleman's Gentleman*, appeared on that list.

When the Queen Mother died in 2002, shortly before her 102nd birthday, and because I am an angler, I was asked to write a few notes about her love of fly-fishing. Fly-fishing is a universal pleasure that transcends the boundaries of age, race, class or creed. It brings together people from all walks of life who share common interests: a deep love of the countryside, respect for their quarry and consideration for the aspirations of others.

Few anglers expressed these sentiments more graciously than the Queen Mother, who was one of the world's best known and best loved fly-fishers. However, the Queen Mother was not only a keen angler, but also active in promoting the best interests of the sport. For many years, she was the Patron of the Salmon & Trout Association, a position that is now filled by His Royal Highness Prince Charles, who, as a youth, was much influenced by his grandmother's love of fishing.

When the Queen Mother purchased Barrogill Castle in 1952, she restored the castle's name to its ancient title, Castle of Mey. The castle had been built in the later years of the sixteenth century by George Sinclair, 4th Earl of Caithness, and remained in the hands of the Sinclair family until 1889. The Queen Mother discovered Barrogill Castle on a visit to her friends, Commander Clair Vyner and his wife, Lady Doris, who lived at the House of the Northern Gate on the cliffs of Dunnet Head, the most northerly point on Mainland Scotland.

Looking east from one of the upper floor windows of the house one day, the Queen Mother noticed the tower of the castle. It had recently been put on the market by the then owner, Captain Imbert-Terry, of the York family who produce the famous chocolates that still bear his name. After visiting Barrogill, the Queen Mother bought it and set about the considerable task of modernising the property.

The Queen Mother spent many happy months in Caithness over nearly fifty years. She loved the remote lochs of the Caithness Flow Country where she used to fish for wild brown trout on Loch Caluim on the Dorrery Estate. She also came to know and love the Thurso River and was a frequent guest there, often accompanied by her favourite corgis, Billy and Bee. David Sutherland, the River Superintendent, remembered being with the Queen Mother one day in 1953 when she was fishing with Commander Vyner and Sir Arthur Penn, her then Private Secretary.

He recalled, "The day was calm and thundery and although we saw plenty of fish on the move, none were taking. But this did not deter the Queen Mother. She threw a beautiful line and fished continuously for four hours and enjoyed every minute." The Queen Mother always had a kind word for fellow anglers, sharing stories of ones that got away and the few that didn't. But perhaps the most famous story recounts how a lady angler, fishing the Royal Dee, suddenly discovered that she was sharing a Beat with the

Queen Mother and instinctively curtsied, receiving two bootfuls of icy water in the process.

It was always the Queen Mother's wish that, when she died, her Caithness home should be continued in the way that she had established and nurtured it for nearly half a century. Above all, she was proud of her pedigree herds of Aberdeen Angus cattle and North Country Cheviot sheep. To achieve this, in June 1996, she set up the Queen Elizabeth Castle of Mey Trust and, to secure its future, endowed it with the castle, farm and estate. When the castle was opened to the public in August 2002, more than 900 visitors were welcomed on the first day. Today, the castle receives upwards of 25,000 visitors each year and employs fifty people during the season.

Along with King George VI, the Queen Mother had been patron of the Aberdeen Angus Cattle Society since 1937 and, after her husband's death, she remained patron for the rest of her life. The Castle of Mey Aberdeen Angus Herd was established in 1964 and soon began to produce a long succession of magnificent animals and show-winners, including, and perhaps the most outstanding, Castle of Mey Elscot, which sold at the Perth Bull sales in 1996 for the then record price of 8,000gns.

The Queen Mother was also patron of the North Country Cheviot Sheep Society and the Longoe Flock was established in 1960. Sheep from her flock have won Breed Champion awards nine times at the prestigious Royal Highland Show at Ingliston near Edinburgh. The most famous wins, however, came in 1991 and 1996. In 1991, the shearling ewe, Longoe H3, not only won the breed champion award, but also went on to win the Supreme Interbreed Sheep champion award out of 2,500 entries, as well as the coveted Queen's Cup – thus, her daughter's trophy was presented to the Queen Mother by her granddaughter, Her Royal Highness Princess Anne. In 1996, at the fiftieth anniversary show of the North Country Sheep Society, the shearling ram, Longoe Majestic, took top place out of 254 entries.

I came to know the Castle of Mey in the 1970s, when I was manager of an agricultural land drainage company. The Queen Mother's factor, Martin Leslie, asked me to look at some land drainage problems at the castle and at the farm. The farm was managed by the late Donald McCarthy and when he died, his sons, Donald and Sandy, took over the management of the farm. Donald was a good friend of my daughter, Lewis-Ann, and they had been at agricultural college together.

I called in December to speak to Donald about the Aberdeen Angus cattle and North Country Cheviot sheep that his family had looked after for so many years. We sat in the farmhouse kitchen over a cup of coffee, where the Queen Mother had often sat, and Donald told me, "She was a great person with a wonderful sense of humour. We miss her. When she died, it seemed strange – the castle open to the public and all these people walking about. But it is what she wanted. She loved having the cattle and sheep round the castle, seeing them from her window, and she knew a good animal when she saw one. After a show or sale, she was always waiting by the phone to hear the result and was delighted if we had taken a prize."

The farm is half a mile from Castle of Mey but well into her nineties, the Queen Mother used to walk along the shore by the Pentland Firth to visit the farm. I asked Donald what his fondest memories of her were; he smiled and said, "I think it was her coming in here, when she was home in August for about six weeks. She would come down two or three times and sit in that chair and yarn away. I think that she enjoyed a good yarn, on lots of different topics, a total contrast from her life in London. She could get on old clothes here and walk wherever she wanted. Nobody bothered her."

The President of the Queen Elizabeth Castle of Mey Trust is the Queen Mother's grandson and heir to the throne, HRH Prince Charles, Duke of Rothesay. He has carried forward his grandmother's wishes for the Castle of Mey and shares her love of Caithness. During the 1980s, when inappropriate commercial forestry was claiming thousands of acres of the irreplaceable peat moorlands known as the Flow Country, I became involved in an action to protect the area. At the height of the controversy, dubbed by the press as the Battle of the Flows, those of us who were carrying on the fight were enormously encouraged to see Prince Charles on television, in the heart of the Flow Country, patiently explaining why these moorlands deserved to be preserved.

HRH Prince Charles was also a positive influence in establishing what has become one of the great Caithness success stories of recent years, the development of North Highland Products; a company formed to look after and develop the exclusive brand name Mey Selections, which sources high-quality products from local farmers and fine-food producers. I called to speak to Danny Miller, the chairman of North Highland Products, who farms at Bilbster, near Wick, and asked him how the local farming community benefited from the initiative. Danny said, "Mey Selections provides a top-quality product and also guarantees a premium to our farmers. Our customers know that, by buying Mey Selections products, a little bit more money is going back into the wider local community."

Danny, who was the local National Farmers Union chairman at the time, knew that Prince Charles was keen to help and drew together a group of thirteen Caithness farmers who put up £300 each to fund a feasibility study. The study suggested that brand promotion was the way forward. The Prince responded by offering a watercolour that he had painted of the Castle of Mey and agreed that they could use the painting as their company logo. Danny told me, "We launched in 2005 and, very quickly, the national supermarket group Sainsbury's came on board, selling our beef from their butchery counters, and, shortly thereafter, Mey Selections lamb as well."

Today, Mey Selections has seventy-five products in its range, from Barrogill Whisky to tweeds, jams, conserves, pickles, chutneys, biscuits, honey, oatcakes, cheese, beef and lamb, all produced within 100 miles of the Castle of Mey, and all subject to stringent and carefully monitored quality-control procedures. From the original thirteen farmers, the group has now expanded and includes nearly 500 members. From start-up funding of £4,000, turnover has grown to £11 million.

Danny Miller is certain that North Highland Products will continue to grow and prosper, and of the key role that HRH Prince Charles played in its foundation. He said, "Fundamental to this success is the initiative that Prince Charles brought to the project. He gave us the confidence we needed to take the first step." North Highland Products is probably the fastest growing food and drink company in Scotland and regularly wins Excellence Awards for its products. See: www.mey-selections.com/ for details. For online-ordering, email: info@mey-selections.com

Prince Charles has also carried on the tradition of attending the Mey Highland Games, held in August each year at Queen's Park, Mey. The Prince and his wife, Camilla, Duchess of Cornwall, who were married in 2005, have visited the games each year. The games grew out of the Queen Mother's suggestion that a tug-of-war competition should be held between the Castle of Mey staff and a team from the local branch of the Royal British Legion. HRH Prince Charles is the Honorary President of the games, which include Heavy Events, Track and Field events, Solo Piping and Highland Dancing.

One of the "mainstays" of the Mey Games is Charlie Simpson from Wick, who has been a member of the Royal British Legion for more than fifty years. A remarkable, multi-talented man, Charlie was, until not so long ago, a regular and successful competitor in the Heavy Events, not only at Mey, but also around the whole Highland Games circuit. Charlie is also an accomplished public speaker, always in demand for Burns Suppers and other special occasions, and plays a wide range of musical instruments. I have known Charlie for more than twenty-five years and, on occasions, had the pleasure of sharing a platform with him at Wick Burns Suppers.

The Mey Games attract more than 1,000 visitors and funds raised by the event are distributed to the Erskine Homes, which care for ex-servicemen and women, and local charities also benefit. I called to see Charlie and asked him how he became involved in the games. "I always had an interest in them but when I was in the Royal Air Force [RAF], my primary sport was boxing – won the Command Championships in 1952 and boxed for the RAF at the Royal Albert Hall. When I was home on leave in 1954, the Wick Games were on, so I went down and entered the shot-put event and won the competition. So, when I came out of the RAF, I just carried on, going to games throughout the Highlands and enjoying every minute of it."

Charlie's involvement with the Mey Games came about when the Mey Branch of the Legion asked him to join. Charlie, whose parents lived in Mey, was a policeman and he captained the Queen Mother's tug-of-war team, thus beginning an association with the Queen Mother and her family that lasts to this day. The 2008 Mey Games were held in appalling weather conditions – cold, with heavy rain. Nevertheless, Prince Charles and his wife attended, particularly to watch the tug-of-war event.

For reasons we need not go into here, the vital rope was missing and Charlie had to break the news to his Royal visitors. "I had to tell Prince Charles that the rope was missing, that it was a wee bit technical, but that there could be no tug-of-war. I suggested they would be a lot warmer in the Castle. 'Does that mean we can go?' 'Yes,' I said. 'Thank goodness for that,' replied the Prince."

Charlie has fond memories of the Queen Mother, of her kindness and courtesy to all she met. Charlie told me, "After the tug-of-war, both teams were entertained for lunch at the Castle. The Queen Mother always came along to say hello. She just seemed to know everybody and spoke to everybody. She was a very lovely person."

I left the library and made my way down the imposing staircase to the front door of the castle. The hall is furnished with many pieces the Queen Mother bought from two shops in Thurso – Miss Miller Calder's shop and Hettie Munro's shop, the Ship's Wheel; both shops were first-stop calls for the Queen Mother for tea and to catch up on all the local gossip. The Queen Mother may be gone but her memory will always be bright in the Far North. When the sun shines kindly on the Castle of Mey, Charlie Simpson always used to call it a "Queen Mother's day". That is how she is remembered in Caithness, like a sunny day.

37.
Pentland Firth Lifeboats,
"For Those in Peril on the Sea"

The wave crashed into our boat with enormous fury. As the bow climbed above it, a vast plume of spray engulfed the vessel. I stood, wedged into a tight corner on the upper deck, with my young son, Blair, clutched against my body. Astern, the lights from Scrabster Harbour in Caithness winked and faded. Ahead lay a boiling seascape of tormented blue and white water. In the distance, I glimpsed the faint outline of the red-scarred cliffs of the Island of Hoy.

The incident happened on a stormy day in 1967 when we sailed from Scrabster to Stromness in Orkney on a family holiday. This was my first meeting with one of the most famously wild seas in the world, the Pentland Firth, the narrow passage of between ten to thirteen kilometres in width that separates Mainland Scotland from the Orkney Isles. The turbulence that gives it such a fearsome reputation is caused by the clash of the Atlantic Ocean greeting the North Sea.

Many years later, I decided that I should meet some of the people who risked their lives going to the assistance of vessels in distress: the men and women of the Royal National Lifeboat Institution (RNLI), one of the most remarkable organisations in the world and whose crew members give of their time on an entirely voluntary basis.

There are forty-five RNLI stations round Scotland's shores, five of which cover the Pentland Firth area: at Wick, to the south of the firth, Thurso, operating out of Scrabster Harbour in Thurso Bay, in Orkney at Stromness in the south west, Kirkwall on Scapa Flow and at Longhope on the south east of the Island of Hoy. Last year, these five stations alone launched sixty times and saved the lives of sixty-nine people.

The Pentland Firth fills and drains the North Sea twice a day. Three million tonnes of water surge through the channel every second, from the Atlantic to the North Sea and back again. Even on a calm day, when the tide is flowing from east to west, enormous waves build up off the Caithness coast near the Castle of Mey. This display of unbridled power is known to mariners and locals as "The Merry Men of Mey" and often extends to engulf the whole of the firth.

I thought of the "Merry Men" as I crossed the firth to meet Fred Breck, coxswain of the Stromness lifeboat. Fred lectures at Orkney College, part of the University of the Highlands and Islands, and I found him at their premises near the harbour, where schoolchildren were being introduced to the basics of small boat handling.

Fred has been coxswain now for four years. There are seventeen crewmembers and every member has a pager. When the call comes, day or night, they hurry to the station. On a call, or "shout" as it is known, seven of the crew are selected to man the boat. The coxswain chooses them depending upon the type of situation involved.

Most of the Stromness crew has seafaring backgrounds and Fred himself has spent much of his working life at sea and, on one occasion in 1989, in it. He was washed over the stern during a gale when his fishing boat was retrieving its nets. All he could see when he came to the surface was the boat going full speed away from him. Fortunately, the skipper, who knew that water had come onboard, looked out of the wheelhouse and saw him, bobbing up and down in the distance.

Fred told me, "I couldn't keep up with the motion of the sea. The waves were coming over the top of me. When I went under, I was looking up, like this, ye ken, and I could see the disk of the sun. Then I would come to the surface again and gasp in some air. A kind of amusing thing was that there were wee gulls, swimming around me, wondering what's this in the water here, you know?"

The boat came back and a lifebelt was thrown. Fred grabbed it, and thought, "I'm bloody sure I'm not letting go. I have never worked so hard in my life to stay alive." Fred told me he had once been fishing about fifteen miles to the west of the Fair Isles, between Orkney and Shetland, when the hold of the boat he was working on accidentally flooded. Disaster was averted when the Lerwick lifeboat came to their aid. "I suppose," Fred said, "that by joining the lifeboat crew, I felt that I was giving something back to those who had helped me. I have never regretted doing so."

Kevin Davidson has been a crewmember of the Thurso lifeboat for eighteen years and lives in Scrabster, close to the lifeboat station at the harbour. He works in the ambulance and fire service at Dounreay Atomic Power Station but has always been fascinated by the sea. His uncle, William Farquhar, was coxswain for nineteen years (he was in the crew for thirty-three years) and, in 1999, received the RNLI Bronze Medal for service to a burning chemical tanker, *Multitank Ascania*, when dangerously close inshore at Dunnet Head.

I asked Kevin if the possibility of a call out ever preyed on his mind: "Not really," he replied, "perhaps on a bad winter night, but once out the only thing that really matters is concentrating on the job in hand." Kevin gave me a conducted tour of the Thurso boat *The Taylors* and during the tour, Thurso coxswain, William "Wing" Munro joined us. I asked him why he became involved with the lifeboat. Glancing at Kevin, he replied, "Well, it's better than being a fireman and ambulance man at Dounreay!" This humour and shared sense of comradeship was evident in everyone I met.

Although I didn't have the opportunity of visiting the Kirkwall and Longhope lifeboat stations, I was enormously impressed by their achievements. In January 1984, Coxswain William Swanson Sinclair was awarded a RNLI Bronze Medal when his lifeboat, during a storm with driving snow and very rough seas, saved the lives of three members of a fishing boat that had become stranded amongst rocks. In 2000, the Kirkwall lifeboat, in a severe gale and six-metre-high waves, used their knowledge of tides to search for and rescue a diver found sixteen kilometres away from his last known position.

The Longhope lifeboat also has an illustrious record of service. Last year, Dr Christine Bradshaw was awarded the RNLI Bronze Medal for Gallantry after going out on the Longhope lifeboat, despite not being a regular crewmember, to assist three injured men on the tanker *FR8 Venture*. In hurricane-force winds and huge seas, completely white with foam and spray, she was winched from the lifeboat onto the tanker. One man was already dead and another had received fatal injuries, but Dr Bradshaw was able to save the third man's life.

The Longhope lifeboat crew, headed by coxswain Kevin Kirkpatrick and the Coastguard helicopter crew, also received a collective Framed Letter of Thanks from the RNLI Chairman for their role in this rescue.

But in March 1969, the Longhope station had suffered one of the worst tragedies in British lifeboat history. Their boat and all of its crew were lost answering a mayday call during one of the most severe storms in the islands. They were Coxswain Daniel Kirkpatrick, Second Coxswain James Johnston, Assistant Mechanic James Swanson, and crewmembers Robert Johnston, John T. Kirkpatrick and Eric McFadyen. A memorial to them stands in Kirkhope Cemetery at South Walls.

My final visit was to Wick Lifeboat Station, where I met Coxswain Ian "Corrie" Cormack. I asked him if there was one "shout" that he particularly remembered and he talked about the night they went to assist a ferry in distress off Duncansby Head near John O'Groats.

The *St Rognvald* was sailing from Shetland to Aberdeen on 5 March 1991 when it was hit by a huge wave off the Stacks of Duncansby. The force of the wave smashed the glass on the bridge and twenty tons of water poured into the vessel. The captain received a massive electric shock and was knocked unconscious (he later made a full recovery) and the electrical systems failed. The ship lost all steering power and although the engines were still running, it was in danger of foundering in the storm.

It was dark when the call came to Wick Lifeboat Station. The crew assembled and Coxswain Walter McPhee set out into a storm-tossed sea with gale-force winds of over sixty miles per hour. Corrie was in the crew that night and told me that the lifeboat had stood by the stricken vessel for ten to eleven hours.

A Royal Air Force helicopter was called in to take off non-essential people from the *St Rognvald*. It flew past, missing both boats in the storm. Wick lifeboat put up a flare to direct the helicopter to their position. The coastguards coordinating the mission from the rescue centre on shore asked the lifeboat what conditions were like, but, in addition to the storm, it was pitch-black and difficult to be accurate. It was a south-east gale and they estimated waves were about 9m in height.

The RAF helicopter broke its entire store of high lines during the difficult manoeuvres involved in lifting passengers from the pitching ship and was replaced by a coastguard helicopter from Sumburgh in Shetland, which completed the task. There were not many people onboard the ferry, its purpose being to take cattle and trucks back and forwards between Aberdeen and Shetland, but twenty passengers were air-lifted to safety.

The RAF helicopter crew said afterwards that they had measured the waves at nearer 15m than 9m. By this time, the *St Rognvald* was barely quarter of a mile from the cliffs between Duncansby and Freswick, but the crew eventually managed to rig up an emergency steering system.

The Wick lifeboat navigated them out to sea, away from the cliffs, and then escorted the *St Rognvald* the few miles south to Sinclair Bay, where the vessel found shelter and safety from the storm. An RNLI "Thanks of the Institution Inscribed on Vellum" plaque was awarded to Coxswain McPhee for his work that night and the crew received RNLI vellum service certificates.

Corrie invited me to join his crew on a training exercise. Lifeboat crews train on a regular basis. The task that evening was to take a salvage pump out to a "sinking" fishing boat so that the crew could pump out sufficient seawater to allow the boat to be towed safely back to harbour. I stood by Corrie on the bridge as he directed the operation and was immensely impressed by the sheer professionalism of the crew. Not much was said and the crewmembers seamlessly carried out their duties.

Ashore again, Corrie told me, "There is a bond between everybody. I don't think that I have ever heard an angry word spoken in all the time I have been here. You are doing something you want to do, not something that you have been press-ganged into doing. I think that is something that people have in them. We are very lucky to have such volunteers because without their commitment, we are nothing."

As I drove homewards, I thought of the many times that I had been intimidated by the strength and fury of the uproarious Pentland Firth, and of the men and women who were ready, every hour of every day and night, to come to my assistance. I felt humbled by their courage and commitment.

The RNLI in Scotland is currently running a "train one, save many" fundraising campaign with the aim of raising £500,000 over the next two years to fund crew training at lifeboat stations around Scotland. For more information please visit, http://www.rnli.org.uk/how_to_support_us/appeals/tosm/ or email: Scotland@rnli.org.uk or call 01738 642999 quoting "Scottish Appeal".

Of the 824 members of lifeboat crews in Scotland, 774 are volunteers, allowing the charity to spend more of its funds on equipment, lifeboats and training. Every RNLI crewmember gives up their own time to undertake 150 hours of competence-based training every year. It costs an average of £1,000 a year to train each volunteer crewmember.

The Royal National Lifeboat Institution charity saves lives at sea. Its volunteers provide a twenty-four-hour search-and-rescue service around the United Kingdom and Republic of Ireland coasts. The RNLI is independent of Coastguard and government, and depends on voluntary donations and legacies to maintain its rescue service.

Since the RNLI was founded in 1824, its lifeboat crews and lifeguards have saved over 137,000 lives.

38.
The Rough Bounds of Knoydart

The small boat was busy and its decks crowded. As we set sail, children and adults chattered and jostled good-humouredly, finding a comfortable space in which to spend the journey. Once clear of the harbour, the Sound of Sleat greeted us with sparkling, blue-bright waves and I thrilled to the feeling of adventure that comes only with the salty scent of sea spray.

Kittiwake, herring gulls and black-backed gulls clustered astern, screaming their approval at our departure. Etched like snow-white flakes on the vast canvas of the silver and gold sky, gannets hovered and dived for fish. Ahead lay our destination, the tiny hamlet of Inverie on the Knoydart Peninsula, forty minutes by boat from Mallaig at the end of the Road to the Isles.

Knoydart is one of Scotland's last great wilderness areas. It enfolds 55,000 acres and lies to the west of Fort William between "heaven and hell"; the names given to the two fjord-like sea lochs, Nevis to the south and Hourn in the north, that guard it. Knoydart has been designated a National Scenic Area for its diversity of flora and fauna and for its outstanding beauty.

It is also known as the "Rough Bounds" because of the majesty of the landscape. Six Munros crown the horizon: Ladhar Bheinn (The Claw Hill), Sgurr na Ciche (The Peak of the Breast), Garbh Chioch Mhor (The Big Rough Place), Meall Buidhe (The Yellow Hill), Luinne Bheinn (The Hill of Anger) and, across Loch Hourn, Beinn Sgritheall (The Gravel Hill).

Apart from by boat, the only way in is on foot from Strathan at the end of the public road at the head of Loch Arkaig, a taxing sixteen-mile trek. The path climbs through Glen Dessary, amidst the ragged mountains where Bonnie Prince Charlie hid after his defeat at Culloden, to the ruins of Finiskig on the shores of Loch Nevis. The route then winds past Camasrory and Carnoch before climbing steeply through Gleann Meadail and down to the River Inverie.

This was my first visit to Knoydart, the only place in the land I love and call home that I had yet to explore. As our vessel, the *Western Isles*, crossed Loch Nevis, the outline of the few houses lining the shore below the massive bulk of Sgurr Coire Choinnichean took shape and form. On the port side, we passed the dramatic white statue of "Our Lady" on the rocky headland of Rubha Raonuill. A few minutes later, we were alongside the pier at Inverie.

A crowd of people awaited our arrival, to meet friends and visitors, collect supplies shipped over from Mallaig and mainland Scotland – building materials, household goods, food and drink – and all the other necessities that the people who live here depend upon to sustain their lifestyle. Cheerful greetings filled the air as the crew helped their passengers disembark.

The resident population of Knoydart amounts to some sixty people. There is a well-stocked shop, the famous Old Forge Inn – the most remote pub on the UK mainland, a primary school with nine pupils and a nursery school with two. In and around Inverie, there are a number of comfortable self-catering properties and bed-and-breakfast houses amongst the heather and ferns that cover the skirts of the hills.

The early seventeenth centrury saw the MacDonnells in control of Knoydart, but their power and influence faded after their ill-judged support of the Jacobite cause and by the nineteenth century they, like so many of their peers, began to clear the people to make way for sheep. The most fearful of those forced evictions took place in August 1853, when Josephine MacDonnell had 330 people frog-marched onto the vessel *Sillery* to be shipped to Canada.

Eleven families refused to go and some of them fled into the Rough Bounds to hide from the laird's officers and the policemen who assisted them in this brutal act. These people, sixty in number, were hunted down and bundled onboard. A few years later, the MacDonnells sold out to James Baird of Cambusdoon, a successful Ayrshire businessman.

From then onwards, a succession of wealthy individuals used Knoydart as their personal playground, the most infamous being the entirely unlamented Arthur Nall-Cain, 2nd Baron Brocket. Brocket was anti-Semitic and an ardent fan of Nazi Germany. In April 1939, five months before the outbreak of the Second World War, along with Major-General John Fuller and the Duke of Buccleuch, he travelled to Germany to celebrate Hitler's fiftieth birthday.

After the war, in 1948, Brocket again faced reprobation when a group of seven men, including war veterans, raided Knoydart and marked out sixty-five acres of arable land and 10,000 acres of hill land upon which to settle. The "Seven Men", as reported in *The Scotsman* newspaper at the time, were "invoking the Land Settlement Act, which permitted returning servicemen to take over land which was under-used and farm it as their own".

Lord Brocket was not amused and applied for a court order to remove them from his land. Hamish Henderson, one of Scotland's most articulate men of letters, wrote about the incident:

"You bloody Reds," Lord Brocket yelled,
"What's this you're doing here?
It doesn't pay, as you'll find today,
To insult an English peer,
You're only Scottish half-wits,
But I'll make you understand.
You Highland swine,
These hills are mine,
This is all Lord Brocket land."

Eventually, backed by government, Brocket won, but the Seven Men of Knoydart achieved a moral victory, which is commemorated to this day by a monument to them erected in Inverie.

The oppressive reign of insensitive landlords came to an end in the 1980s when Surrey property dealer Phillip Rhodes acquired the estate. He began selling off bits of the estate and, in doing so, was, perhaps unwittingly, the catalyst for change. The last 17,000 acres were bought by a jute manufacturing company called Titaghur and when the company went into receivership, the land was acquired by the Knoydart Foundation in a community-led buy-out. This secured the future of the area for the benefit of the people who lived and worked there.

My accommodation in Inverie was a cottage close to the "Seven Men of Knoydart" monument and in the early evening, I wandered out to see what I could see. The bay was mirror calm and several yachts lay peacefully at anchor. The smell of peat smoke filled the air, and I watched as the crews of the yachts bundled themselves into tiny dinghies and rowed ashore. Most of the occupants seemed to be heading for the Old Forge, so I followed them.

Stepping through the door, it was as though I had been transported into an entirely new world. The long bar was thronged with people who were clearly enjoying themselves enormously; two musicians, guitar and violin, were playing and singing lustily, with the rest of the assembled company joining in. At the end of each piece, loud cheers echoed round the room.

The players providing the entertainment were part of a group who had travelled by train from Glasgow, thence on to Inverie. They were mostly climbers and hillwalkers, and they were also celebrating the forthcoming marriage of one of their friends – lustily.

The Old Forge Inn is owned and run by the remarkable Ian and Jacqui Robertson and it is the "hub" of social life in Inverie. Ian told me that most of the 4,000-plus visitors who come to Knoydart each year pass through his doors, and the pub has attracted an astonishing number of accolades and awards, including the "Highlands and Islands Best Visitor Experience" in 2007.

The following morning, I met Drew Harris, the manager of the Kilchoan Estate, the western part of the old Knoydart Estate, which is now run as a sporting and recreational enterprise. I wanted to have a closer look at what the estate had to offer people afflicted with angling and, perhaps, remove a few brown trout from their natural habitat.

Drew is one of those people who does not understand the meaning of the word "impossible", and showed it through his boundless enthusiasm and obvious love for the land he looked after. As an angler, I readily accepted Drew's invitation to explore its waters. I fished remote Loch an Dubh-Lochain for wild brown trout and the delightful little Inverie River for salmon and sea-trout. Loch an Dubh-Lochain lies at the very heart of the Rough Bounds of Knoydart and is, quite simply, magnificent.

The loch is deep, dropping to a depth of almost 30m, and is one mile long by up to 400 yards wide. Look out for pretty wild brown trout that average 8–10oz in weight. But there are much larger specimens as well, including ferox trout, the aquatic "wolf" that is descended from species that have inhabited the loch since the end of the last Ice Age – along with their attendant population of Arctic charr.

Loch an Dubh-Lochain is the headwater loch of the River Inverie, a notable salmon and sea-trout fishery that is recovering from the less than welcome impact of the fish farms in Loch Nevis. Drew Harris of Kilchoan Estate is conducting a re-stocking programme that is beginning to produce encouraging results. In spite of low water levels during my visit, several sea-trout of up to and over 4lb in weight had been caught and released, and salmon parr were abundant.

There are two other trout lochs on the hill to the south of Kilchoan, Loch Bhraomisaig at Gd ref: 785973 and its unnamed satellite lochan to the west on the slopes of Lagan Loisgte. Bhraomisaig lies at about 350m and it might test your lungs a bit getting there, but it holds some excellent trout that can exceed 4lbs in weight. Neither Bhraomisaig nor its satellite surrender their residents easily but, be assured, they are there, waiting for your carefully presented fly.

But the estate is not only about stalking and fishing. It encourages hill walkers and provides first-class bunk-house facilities to accommodate them. There are whale-watching sea trips and visits to remote, uninhabited islands. You may stalk red deer with a camera, and watch otters at play in the river and along the shores of Loch Nevis. Or simply relax in the outstanding comfort of the estate's self-catering cottages. For further information, contact Drew Harris on tel: 01687 462724 or email: drewhkilchoan@onetel.com.

It was hard to leave Inverie but at 11am on a Monday morning, I found myself back on the pier awaiting the arrival of the ferry. As we headed out across Loch Nevis towards Mallaig, I watched the village fade and merge into the backdrop of blue-grey mountains. But I was quite certain that I would be back.

39.
Loch Ness Myths and Monsters

The River Ness runs through the center of "Inversneckie", the affectionate local name given to Inverness, the Scottish Highlands' capital city. Some years ago, I was walking by the banks of the river on a warm September afternoon when a considerable commotion broke out amongst those around me; people crowded the river bank, pointing excitedly to the middle of the stream, cameras clicking furiously.

After several days of heavy rain, the river was in full spate, a brown and white tumbling torrent pouring wildly out of the vastness of Loch Ness. I heard a voice exclaiming, "It's the monster! Look, look, it's the monster!" A huge back arched above the water and then plunged again into the depths. A moment later, the shape reappeared and I identified it as being the back of an enormous salmon.

But what a fish it was, and little wonder that many of the onlookers, who were mostly visitors to the north, instantly thought that they were in fact viewing the fabled Loch Ness Monster. It was impossible to tell accurately, but I estimated that the fish must have been well over 60lbs in weight and, if caught, would certainly have been the largest salmon ever landed in Scottish waters. Even after the fish had disappeared upstream, the excited chatter amongst the bystanders continued.

Scotland is famous for the quality of its salmon fishing and the Ness system is amongst the most famous of them all, on the river, the loch and on its many tributaries. These most sporting of fish return each year from their North Atlantic feeding grounds to spawn in the rivers where they were born, but once they reach Loch Ness, because of its size and depth, they are relatively safe from the ungentle administrations of anglers.

Loch Ness is renowned throughout the world because of the alleged presence of Nessie, the Loch Ness Monster. Nessie shares his/her habitat with eels, pike, stickleback, lamprey, minnows, salmon, sea-trout, brown trout and Arctic charr. The loch is some thirty-seven kilometres long by up to two and a half kilometres wide at its widest point, between Urquhart Castle on the north shore and Whitefield on the south shore. The loch lies in the grasp of the Great Glen Fault, a geological feature that is still attempting to separate the Highlands from Central Scotland. This seismic movement has been active for more than 400 million years and is evidenced by regular earthquakes; well, regular in geological terms, that is, being at the rate of about three quakes every century at level 4 on the Richter scale. The most severe earthquake occurred in 1816 when the impact was felt throughout all of Scotland.

Until the end of the last Ice Age, about 8,000 years ago, Loch Ness was glacier-filled. When the ice melted, the loch was formed and drops to a depth of almost 240m. It contains more water than all of the lakes in England and Wales put together. Loch Ness is the largest of the three lochs in the Great Glen, the other two being Loch Lochy and Loch Oich. All of these waters are linked together by the Caledonian Canal, designed by Thomas Telford to provide a safe and quicker route between Loch Linnhe in the west and the Moray Firth in the east. Work on the near 100-kilometre long project started in 1803 and the original cost was estimated to be £350,000 during a seven-year construction period. However, the construction of the canal took seventeen years and it wasn't completed until 1822 at a final cost of £840,000. There are twenty locks along the length of the canal, the most spectacular being Neptune's Staircase to the north of Fort William near Corpach. This consists of a series of eight locks that raise vessels to a height of twenty metres above sea level over a distance of 500 yards.

I first visited Loch Ness more years ago than I care to remember but I will never forget the impression it made on me then; bounded on either side by blue-grey mountains and seemingly endless; mirror calm one moment, dark and foreboding the next, ever-changing and much of the south shoreline is virtually inaccessible to all but the most determined. I walked on the beach by Dores at the north end of the loch and explored the old woodlands down to Lochend where the Caledonian Canal feeds into the system and the waters from Loch Ness hurry northwards through Loch Dochfour and the River Ness to the sea.

Another, earlier, and equally impressed visitor was Thomas Pennant (1726–1798). This dour Welshman and caustic observer of all things Highland passed this way on his tour of Scotland in 1769. He commented: "In many parts we were immersed in woods; in others, they opened and gave views of the sides and tops of vast mountains soaring above. The wild animals that possessed this picturesque scene were stags and roes, black game and grouse; and on the summits, white hares and ptarmigan. Foxes are so numerous and voracious that the farmers are sometimes forced to house their sheep, as is done in France, for fear of wolves."

The road that Pennant followed then was the only reasonable route south from Inverness down the Great Glen to Fort William. Built by General Wade (1673–1748) in the aftermath of the Jacobite rebellions of 1715 and 1719, Wade's roads were part of a network to facilitate the speedier deployment of troops to control the clans of these unruly northern lands. This tortuous road is now classified as the B852 and it parallels the south shore of the loch through Inverfarigaig to the village of Foyers. From Foyers, a well-ordered path leads steeply down to a viewpoint overlooking dramatic falls on the River Foyers; an over forty-metre-high waterfall that thunders into a spectacular gorge and leads to Loch Ness.

Scotland's bard, Robert Burns, visited the falls in 1787 and immortalised them in verse:

Among the healthy hills and ragged woods
The roaring Fyers pours his mossy floods,
Till full he dashes on the rocky mounds,
Where, thro' a shapeless breach, his stream resounds.

As high in air the bursting torrents flow,
As deep recoiling surges foam below,
Prone down the rock the whitening sheet descends,
And viewless Echo's ear, astonished, rends.

Dim-seen, through rising mists and ceaseless show'rs,
The hoary cavern wide surrounding lours:
Still thro' the gap the struggling river toils,
And still, below, the horrid cauldron boils.

Burns never mentioned the monster or Loch Ness but since early times the story has persisted. St Columba arrived from Iona in the sixth century, determined to persuade the heathen Picts to mend their ways. During his visit, he is said to have saved one of his companions, who was swimming in the River Ness, from being eaten by a fierce water monster. St Columba made the sign of the cross in the air and, in a loud voice, demanded that the monster depart, which it immediately did, thus saving the life of the terrified, floundering monk.

My own view is that the monster does exist. I don't know what kind of creature it might be but I am sure that there is something there. Indeed, I knew a young man, born and bred in Inverness, who claimed to have seen it early one morning when he was camping by the shores of the loch. His description followed similar accounts of sightings of the monster, in as much as the creature was several hundred yards offshore and glimpsed only briefly. But he recounted that it had a long neck, high above the level of the water, and that it appeared to have a long tail. I never drive along the new Inverness/ Fort William road on the north shore of the loch without keeping a weather eye open for Nessie, and I am pretty sure that most other people passing that way do the same.

One morning in May, a friend and I stopped by Urquhart Castle on the north shore to take a few pictures and generally see what we could see. "I'll let you know when I spot the monster," I announced confidently, because

Urquhart Bay has probably been the source of more sightings of the monster than anywhere else on the loch. However, the surface of the water remained stubbornly undisturbed by anything other than sudden gusts of wind and pleasure boats trailing long, white, ever-widening wakes behind them. But it was a wonderful morning and the ancient red sandstone castle on Strone Point looked magnificent. It was inhabited for centuries, by the Picts in the first millennium and thereafter by successive Clan Fraser lairds until 1689. Then, to deny its security to similarly-minded rebel forces in the future, before leaving, they blew up much of the castle and left it largely in the condition that visitors see today.

My purpose that morning lay at the end of the loch, at Fort Augustus, and we sped along the A82, through Invermoriston and Port Clair to reach our destination in goodly time for a previously arranged appointment. The name, Fort Augustus, owes its existence to the disaster that befell the area in the aftermath of the defeat of Prince Charlie's Jacobite army at Culloden on Wednesday, 16 April 1716. The battle was over in about half an hour and by midday, more than 2,000 of the Prince's followers lay dead or dying on Drumossie Moor near Inverness. The rest, including their "Bonnie" commander, were flying in disarray or lying helpless on the field of battle waiting for Cumberland's eager bayonets to end their misery. Fort Augustus became the command center for the "cleaning up" operation when Cumberland's troops raped and ravaged the surrounding countryside.

Today, Fort Augustus is an attractive, busy, welcoming town that plays host to the thousands of visitors that arrive each year to explore Loch Ness. I hoped to do the same and was excitedly looking forward to being afloat on Scotland's most famous water. I was to do so through the courtesy of a business that has been taking care of its guests for nearly fifty years, Cruise Loch Ness run by Ronald Mackenzie, whose father founded the company. Their boats are berthed at a jetty in the centre of town, below the Caledonian Canal swing bridge and next to the Clansman Centre.

I reported to Marcus Atkinson, the manager of Cruise Loch Ness, and he outlined what he planned for the visit. Marcus is a Cornishman and sailing instructor who had spent most of his life working in the Mediterranean. He arrived in the Great Glen in 1994 on a six-month summer contract, met his future wife, a local girl, and has been in Fort Augustus ever since. Nor does he have any intention of leaving. "It is a wonderful place to live and in which to bring up a family. Even although it is always busy during the summer months, there is still a great sense of community. We know most people and most people know us. I can't think of a better place to be and I have the best job in the world," he said.

Cruise Loch Ness offers their clients two distinct trips on Loch Ness: on a traditional vessel, *The Royal Scot*, a beautifully maintained and equipped boat with excellent facilities – lounge, bar, comfortable view areas – crewed by attentive, courteous and knowledgeable staff, most of whom live locally. *The Royal Scot* can also be booked for private functions, wedding receptions, anniversary celebrations and corporate entertaining purposes. The other option is to enjoy the experience of an hour or so afloat in a RIB; a unique, fast and exhilarating ride in a rigid inflatable boat (Zodiac-style) that can explore and access loch-side areas that are otherwise inaccessible to larger vessels. These boats were an instant success when Cruise Loch Ness introduced them a few years ago and are the only vessels of their type on the loch.

I quickly found out the truth of the "fast and exhilarating" bit of the description of a ride in a RIB. Within minutes of our arrival, I was kitted out in all-over wet-weather gear, complete with life jackets and goggles to protect my eyes from flying spray, and speeding down the loch at around thirty-five miles per hour. It was a magical experience; the great loch lay before us, sunlit and sparkling, and a majestic osprey circled overhead. We flew past the only island in Loch Ness, Cherry Island, in a sheltered bay close to the shore north of Fort Augustus. The island is in fact artificial, being a man-made crannog; easily defended structures that were built and inhabited some 5,000 years ago and were still in use until late medieval times. We turned homewards as dark clouds gathered over the peaks in the Glengarry and Aberchalder Forests, and arrived at the jetty thoroughly delighted with all that we had seen on the loch.

As night settled on the great loch, I drove home past a now darkened and sleeping Urquhart Castle and Invermoriston, where the busy river of that name bustles under an old bridge into the bay. Just to the north of Drumnadrochat, I glanced over the loch towards Whitefield. I thought that I saw in the gloaming a commotion on the surface of the loch, far out and barely distinguishable. What could it be? I turned to ask my friend but he was asleep. Whatever, I know that it had been something unusual but what it was I would never know.

Contact Cruise Loch Ness at Cruise Loch Ness, Knockburnie, Inchnacardoch, Fort Augustus, Inverness-shire, PH32 4BN; Tel: 01320 366277; Email: info@ cruiselochness.com; Website: http://www.cruiselochness.com/

40.
Strathnaver and the River of a Thousand Tears

One of the most inauspicious places in all of Scotland for a vehicle to break down is along the narrow, single-track, lonely road between Strath Helmsdale and Strathnaver. When I was a boy, late on an April-sharp afternoon with snow still dusting the top of Ben Klibreck, my father's car did just that during a journey from Edinburgh in the south to Bettyhill at the mouth of the River Naver in North Sutherland.

We huddled in the car whilst Father poked about, less than hopefully, under the bonnet. After an hour's grunting, things were getting desperate. Suddenly, as steely evening approached, an old man appeared riding a rusty old bicycle followed by a rusty old sheep dog. He stopped and asked Father if he could be of any assistance.

The Good Samaritan peered at the innards of the engine for a moment and fiddled under the bonnet. "Now," he said, "just you give it a turn when I give you the signal." Father returned to the driving seat but we could tell from the expression on his face that he considered the matter to be a lost cause. "Now!" came the command.

Father turned the key in the ignition and the engine sprang to life, whirring vigorously and sounding as healthy and as happy as a new-born lamb. Relieved, Father tried to reward our benefactor, who politely refused. "You must be a mechanic?" Father inquired. "Oh, no," came the reply. "I am a Mackay from Strathnaver."

The people of Clan Mackay have lived in Strathnaver for almost 1,000 years and the evidence of their tenure fills the glen; the tumbled stones of their townships and hard-won fields; the place where the 93rd Highlanders regiment was raised; Donald Macleod's monument near to the ruins of the township of Rossal, cleared of its tenants by Patrick Sellar in 1814 during the cruel Strathnaver evictions. Macleod wrote later:

> I was present at the pulling down and burning of the house of William Chisholm in which was lying his wife's mother, an old, bed-ridden woman of nearly one hundred years of age. I told Sellar that the old lady was too ill to be moved. "Damn her!" Sellar replied. "The old witch, she has lived too long, let her burn!" The old woman's daughter arrived whilst the house was on fire and assisted the neighbours in moving her mother out of the flames and smoke, presenting a picture of such horror which I shall never forget . . . she died within five days.

Betsy Mackay was born at Skail, in the middle of Strathnaver, near the old Neolithic burial chamber in the little birch wood. She remembered that Sellar had burned the hill to prepare the land for sheep, destroying spring grazing for the cattle, and that the beasts had wandered far in search of food. Her sister, who had just given birth, was one of the first to be evicted. They lived in the township of Grumore on the shores of Loch Naver. When she asked Patrick Sellar where they should go, he replied that they could go where they liked, so long as it was not Strathnaver.

Bell Cooper lived at Achness, "the cornfield by the cascade", where the tumbling River Mallart meets the River Naver. She remembered children crying all night on the bare hill, watching the smoldering ruins of their homes. Grace Macdonald of Langdale was nineteen years old when her family was burned out. "There was no mercy or pity shown to young or old. All had to clear away and those who could not get their effects removed to a safe distance had them burnt before their eyes."

The architect of the Clearances was an Edinburgh lawyer named James Loch, Commissioner for the Sutherland Estates. He claimed that,

"The adoption of the new system, by which mountainous districts are converted into sheep pastures, even if it should unfortunately occasion the emigration of some individuals, is, upon the whole, advantageous to the nation at large."

The "some individuals" amounted to more than 15,000 men, women and children, evicted from their ancient homes to make way for sheep so that Loch's masters, the Sutherland family, already amongst the most wealthy families in Europe, could become even more wealthy. Patrick Sellar, their Factor, was the compassionless instrument by which the new system was put into effect.

The best place to begin your journey of discovery down Strathnaver is at the museum at Farr Church near Bettyhill. It was in this church that the Rev. Hugh Mackenzie urged his flock to quit without fuss. He told them, "The truly pious acknowledge the mighty hand of God in the matter. In the sight of God, they humble themselves and receive the chastisement of his hand." Mackenzie received rather more for his support of the Duke: a fine manse and the best ground.

Farr Museum displays an account of the Strathnaver Clearances, largely prepared by the children of Farr School. By spending time in the museum, you will be better able to understand the magnitude of the human suffering that the Clearances caused. The museum is dominated by the imposing pulpit from which Mackenzie preached his sycophantic sermon and, propped against the wall, almost unnoticed and dust-covered, is one of the few surviving portraits of Patrick Sellar himself.

Strathnaver was populated before the arrival of Clan Mackay and these earlier people, Mesolithic hunter-gatherers, Neolithic and Iron Age tribes, Picts and others, have left behind them a wide range of monuments and artifacts. The Farr Stone, lying against the west wall of Farr Museum, for example, is a glorious, finely carved, Pictish symbol stone that probably dates back to before the ninth century.

Across the mouth of the River Naver at Bettyhill, partly hidden in the sands of a raised beach, there are the outlines of no less than twenty-six Neolithic hut circles, occupied some 4,500 years ago, and on a hill overlooking settlements stands the ruins of the first of the famous Strathnaver brochs. The sites of these brochs zig-zag south up the river from Invernaver past Loch Naver to Mudale, a distance of twenty-three miles.

The brochs were built over a relatively brief period of time, from approximately 200 BC until AD 100, and their true purpose remains a mystery. They were massive, dry-stone structures, nine to twelve metres in height, enclosing an area of some twelve metres in diameter. The double walls were four and a half metres thick, containing a circular staircase. There was only one small, easily defended entrance. The Romans never invaded Sutherland; the brochs were in place before the Vikings attacked the Scottish coast. Why these massive defensive forts were needed is a matter of pure speculation.

At the east side of the iron bridge over the River Naver, drive south for half a mile to the ruins of the township of Achanlochy, which lie on the hill above Lochan Duinte. There were eight families living at Achanlochy when it was cleared in the spring of 1819, forty-nine souls in all – forty-two of whom shared the same surname, Mackay.

The most extensive post-clearance ruins are at Rossal, further down the strath near Syre, where Patrick Sellar set himself up in a grand house from which he administered the 75,000 acres he eventually rented from the Sutherland Estate; a reward for the results of his efforts on their behalf. A well-marked route leads round the remains of Rossal and there are informative display panels describing how the people lived.

Stop also at the 93rd Highlanders monument. In 1800, when the call came for volunteers, within twenty-four hours 2,000 men had responded. Two hundred and fifty of them were from Strathnaver and 104 were named William Mackay. The Countess of Sutherland promised them "her protection in all time coming and provision for their sons upon their return home". The reality was eviction and destitution.

During the Crimean War, when the cry went up for more "cannon-fodder" for the British Army, the Duke of Sutherland himself hurried north to drum up recruits. There was not a single volunteer. An old man told the Duke why: "How could you expect to find men where they are not? But one comfort you have. Though you cannot find men to fight, you can supply those who will fight with plenty of mutton, beef and venison."

Today, a new breed of laird rules the strath: absentee landlords, devoted to their private preserve of salmon fishing in the river and deer stalking on the hill. The ancient lands of Clan Mackay have been stolen from the people. But in spite of everything, the Mackays have survived and they will still greet you with gentle Highland courtesy, proud to proclaim, "I am a Mackay from Strathnaver."

41.

The 93rd Sutherland Highlanders
and "the Thin Red Line"

I sat at a green baize-covered table in the library of Stirling Castle. Beside me lay a tumble of books and folders containing artifacts and documents from one of Scotland's most illustrious regiments, the 93rd Sutherland Highlanders. The coffee in my cup was untouched and cold. As the December day eased towards evening, embracing the grey walls of the ancient fortress in gathering darkness, I turned the final page and wondered: what land makes such men, what nation deserves such trust?

In May 1800, with snow still clinging to the high tops of Ben Klibreck, Major-General David Douglas Wemyss and Major Gordon Clunes of Cracaig cantered up the banks of the Helmsdale River through the spring-awakened Strath of Kildonan. Their purpose was to raise a regiment of Highlanders to reinforce Britain's canon-fodder-hungry army, depleted by the recent ferocious battles against the French in Europe.

The men they sought were sons of the tenants of the Countess of Sutherland; prior to Wemyss' arrival, a survey had been carried out by the Countess' Ground Officer, Donald Bruce, of the "disposable population" living on her land. These men were summoned to parade before the recruiting officers and reminded of the duty they owed to their Clan Chief and to their Sovereign, King George III.

But hidden behind this patriotic appeal was a threat. Tenants who refused to give up their sons would be evicted. To encourage recruitment, the Countess promised "her protection in all time coming and provision for their sons on their return home". Few came home. Those who did soon discovered the truth of their Chief's fine words: empty straths, cleared of people to make way for more profitable sheep.

As spring lengthened into summer, the recruiting parades continued throughout the Countess' vast domain. In the Parish of Farr at the mouth of the River Naver, men were selected by drawing white and black balls from a box. Murdo Macdonald's two brothers each drew black balls and had to enlist. By mid-August, General Wemyss had his canon-fodder. Shortly thereafter, the call came and 600 young men tramped south to assemble at Fort George near Inverness.

For almost 300 years since then, the Regiment has fought Britain's battles, one of the most notable being the Battle of Balaclava on 25 October 1854, where the 93rd formed the famous "thin red line" to receive a furious Russian cavalry charge. As they waited for their guests to arrive, Sir Colin Campbell, the commander of the Highland Brigade, shouted: "There is no retreat from here, men, you must die where you stand."

"Aye, Sir Colin, and needs be we'll do that," they replied.

One of the greatest disasters to befall the 93rd occurred in 1815 at the Battle of New Orleans. The peace that had existed between Great Britain and America since the end of the War of Independence was shattered by a dispute over which country had been responsible for a sea-fight between a British man-of-war and an American battleship. Britain decided to teach the colonists a lesson. The 93rd were embarked, under the command of Major-General Sir John Keane, to take part in an attack on the south coast of America. The assault force assembled on 23 November at Nigril Bay in Barbados and the whole fleet, amounting to some fifty vessels, set sail on 8 December and anchored off Ship Island in the Gulf of Mexico.

The intention was to capture the rich prize of New Orleans by outflanking garrison forts along the Lower Mississippi. By the end of December, the army was established on the Isle aux Pois, a swampy inlet at the east end of the Pearl River, and final orders were given for the attack. A coordinated assault was planned, both frontal and on the left bank of the river, by moving troops up a shallow lagoon and landing them at Bayou Bienvenue. On the night of 7 January, a force of 1,600 men under Col Thornton set off to occupy that position. It was a hazardous affair, the bayou was a boat-width wide and troops had to land by using the boats as a bridge, passing from one to another until they reached the shore.

As this force advanced inland from the tall reeds fringing the bayou, the ground became firmer and soldiers moved more easily through a forest of cypress trees, sugar cane and orange groves. But the element of surprise was lost when pickets, fleeing from Thornton's approach, raised the alarm.

As dawn broke on the morning of 8 January, Major-General Andrew Jackson's 3,600-strong militia was ready, and the defeat of General Pakenham's 12,000 seasoned British troops was at hand. The main attack was to be launched when Col Thornton's column fired a signal rocket to indicate the success of their left-flanking movement, but the main force, for some inexplicable reason, began its advance too early. Lieutenant C. H. Gordon of the 93rd wrote:

The 93rd moved from its bivouac and advanced in close column. As we neared the enemy lines, day began to dawn. By this time, the enemy could perceive us plainly advancing and no sooner got us within 150 yards of their works than a most destructive and murderous fire was opened on our column of round, grape, musketry, rifle and buckshot. Not daunted, however, we continued our advance, which in one minute would have carried us into their ditch, when we received a peremptory order to halt.

This indeed was the moment of trial, the officers and men being mown down by rank, impatient to get at the enemy at all hazard, yet compelled for want of orders to stand still, and neither to advance or retreat, galled as they were by this murderous fire of an invisible enemy. Not a single American soldier did we see that day, they kept charging their muskets and rifles without lifting their faces above the parapet, the fire from their muzzles being only visible over the parapet.

Meanwhile, Col Thornton and his men pushed on and stormed Morgan's Redoubt and fired the signal rocket; whereupon the American commander, Paterson, spiked his guns and retired, being pursued for about two miles by Thornton's party until the theory of the main attack caused the latter to halt. Thornton himself was wounded and had eighty-three other ranks killed and wounded. He secured the only trophy brought back by this expedition, a small American flag.

Captain Simpson, a naval officer wounded and captured by the defending force, wrote: "Having remained during the whole day in the American field hospital, I had an opportunity of observing the consternation caused to my enemy by Col Thornton's attack on the opposite bank, which was totally unexpected. Conceive my indignation on looking round to find the two leading regiments had vanished as if the earth had opened and swallowed them up."

Col Lambert, who assumed command when General Pakenham was killed, held a council of war. Taking into consideration that a third of the army on the left bank had been killed or wounded and another third was unfit for further fighting, and the danger that Thornton's detachment might be cut off, he ultimately sent a flag of truce to ask for a suspension of hostilities to bury the dead and collect the wounded. Jackson granted an armistice until noon on 9 January. After dark, Lambert, having destroyed his heavy guns, withdrew his troops to the bivouac of the previous night.

An unknown eyewitness of the battle – from the American side – observed, "According to the evidence available, when General Lambert rode forward to assume command, standing in the center, 100 yards from the enemy were the 93rd, proud, eager, helpless and enduring; the only corps which had kept its formation. And we can understand how it was that to the exalting Americans the 93rd Highlanders appeared as firm and immovable as a brick wall."

In later years, the daughter of one of the American defenders recounted in a letter to Lt Col Nightingale of the 93rd: "I have often heard my father say that both officers and men gave proof of the most intrepid gallantry and that it moved him to tears as he saw man after man of the magnificent Highlanders mowed down by the murderous artillery and rifle balls. After the battle, my father took a bible from the body of one of the Highlanders. It had his name but no address and had been given him by his mother."

The 93rd lost 568 men, three-quarters of their strength. The Highlanders lie buried on the field of battle, their final resting place still marked by a grove of cypress trees. Murdo Macdonald's two brothers, who had drawn the black balls at Farr, died together, side by side. The greatest tragedy was that the battle could have been avoided. A preliminary peace treaty was signed on 14 December 1814 and, had news of this been sent promptly to the opposing forces, the battle need never have happened.

The 93rd's Colours, carried during the battle, have a place of honour in Stirling Castle, the present Headquarters of the Regiment, and I paid silent tribute to them before thanking the staff for their courtesy. They told me that a letter had arrived at the Castle that morning from a descendant of one of those who had taken part in the battle – apologising for the unnecessary deaths of so many brave Highlanders.

As I drove north to my home in "Duthaich Mhic Aoidh" – the land of Clan Mackay – I said a prayer for the souls of these Sutherland men and for those who have followed so honorably in their footsteps.

42.
The Black Isle

The Black Isle encapsulates everything that is precious to me about the Scotland I love. It may not have the rugged grandeur of other Highland areas, but for me it irrevocably marries the land to the people who live and work there. It is a peninsula, not an island, separating the Moray Firth in the south from the Cromarty Firth to the north. During winter months, the Black Isle is often snow-free when the rest of Easter Ross and Inverness-shire is blanketed white, hence the name "Black Isle". Until recent times, residents and visitors relied mostly upon passage by sea to get to and from the Black Isle. Ferries were a vital mode of transport amidst the fjord-like coastline of Easter Ross.

However, not everyone was impressed by the safety or efficiency of these vessels. One notable ferry user, Lord Henry Cockburn, an Edinburgh High Court Circuit Judge who traveled the far north administering justice during the nineteenth century, had this to say about Highland ferries: "They are disgraceful! Passengers, cattle and carriages are just lifted and thrown into clumsy, crazy boats, and jerked by bad rowers with unsafe oars, amidst a disorderly tumult of loud, discordant, half-naked and very hairy Celts, who, however, expecting whisky, are at least civil."

Even today, one small, two-car ferry remains, plying between Cromarty and Nigg on the north shore of the Cromarty Firth, although travelers are more comfortably catered for now than they were in 1825. Back then, according to contemporary reports, "Passengers on the Cromarty Ferry had to be carried ashore on a woman's back at the Nigg side."

The most important ferry was at Kessock, sailing between Inverness and the Black Isle. Boats serviced this route from the early years of the fifteenth century. The ferry survived until the building of the Kessock Bridge in 1982, when, "On the final trip to North Kessock, the two ferries were accompanied by small sailing craft, a wind surfer, water skier and a canoeist. Pipe Major Andrew Venters played his own specially composed tune, 'Farewell to Kessock Ferry.'"

One of my favourite places in the Black Isle is the raised beach near Eathie on the north shore of the Moray Firth. These beaches were formed 10,000 years ago, when sea levels fluctuated as the last Ice Age retreated, leaving sand and gravel deposits high above the present level of the sea. Here, I retrace the footsteps of the Black Isle's most famous son, Hugh Miller, a stonemason and geologist born in Cromarty in 1802.

Miller's cottage, built in 1711, is the only remaining thatch-roofed dwelling in Cromarty. It is now a museum that recounts the life and work of this humble man. Miller is a hero of mine. He discovered and explored the fossil fish of the Black Isle Syncline, rocks of the Old Red Sandstone period. Make your own pilgrimage to Hugh Miller's fossil beds to discover for yourself the heart and soul of the Black Isle.

A wooden stile near Eathie Mains Farm leads to a track bordered by a field of barley and an old forest. Along the way, you pass the tumbled stones of a ruined croft on the margins of a reed-fringed pond, alive with the buzz of insects. After a few hundred yards, from the top of the cliff, you will see the blue waters of the Moray Firth and the raised beach below.

The track plunges down the cliff face through banks of heather and yellow ragwort to reach the shore at the Eathie salmon-fishing bothy. The view toward Inverness frames the lighthouse-tipped finger of Chanonry Point, where the seventeenth-century prophet, Brahan Seer, was allegedly boiled in a barrel of tar after bearing bad tidings to the Countess of Seaforth about her husband's infidelity.

Across the firth, the gaunt symmetry of Fort George bulks the horizon. The fort was built by the government in the aftermath of Bonnie Prince Charlie's failed uprising in 1745 to help "control and contain" rebellious Highlanders. It has been used as military barracks ever since. The nearby oilrig platform construction yards at Ardersier throw up steel steeples against the sky.

The fossil-beds are a short walk east from Eathie. Hugh Miller worked here more than 100 years ago, but I feel his presence and hear the sharp tap of his busy hammer every time I pass by. The jagged rocks, as old as time itself, are red, black, blue, white and grey, finely weathered into fantastic shapes and patterns. Strange marks scar the surface of the rocks, painting in the imagination a picture of embryonic life struggling from the ocean.

They are, as Hugh Miller described, "calcareous shales, containing hard limey nodules with occasional fragments of primitive armour-plated fish". I have personal experience of Black Isle rocks and soil. When I managed a land drainage company, we installed field drainage systems in more than 1,000 acres around Munlochy. On my days off, I hiked miles over Munlochy cliffs, searching for the elusive herd of wild goats that live there, but never found them. Their forbears could have been introduced to the Black Isle by Neolithic settlers 5,000 years ago. They feed on gorse, heather and leaves – and everything else that takes their fancy. Which is what goats are for.

In winter months, draining the land was cold, hard work, stamping about misty stubble fields, serenaded by visiting flocks of Arctic greylag geese and Icelandic whooper swans. The Black Isle is renowned for its populations of migrants. But during my work, and in spite of the cold, I got to know the Black Isle intimately, from the toes of my muddy boots to my freezing hands, which were invariably encrusted with rich Black Isle soil.

I felt kinship not only with Hugh Miller, but also with my Scottish ancestors who had felt the same soil trickling through their fingers. After the Iron Age, a Pictish tribe, known to the Romans as the Decantae, cultivated these fields. But the Roman advance of AD 79 stopped short of the Black Isle, and the Decantae were left to their own devices until Viking invaders arrived to "absorb" them into a Norse culture.

One of Scotland's least-sung patriots, Andrew de Moray (d. 1297), was born near the fishing village of Avoch on the Black Isle. Don't ask local people the way to Avoch. Nobody will understand you. It is pronounced "auk". While

William Wallace was raising the south of Scotland in opposition to the usurping Edward I of England, de Moray did the same in the north. Wallace and de Moray eventually defeated Edward's forces at the famous Battle of Stirling Bridge, during which de Moray received his "deathbed" wound.

By the end of the thirteenth century, Cromarty, the principal town of the Black Isle at the northeast tip of the peninsula, had been made a Royal Burgh. David I (1080–1153) began the practice of granting towns Burgh status. This gave them important, exclusive trading privileges and, in the case of a Royal Burgh, the right to be represented in the king's councils. The town was the main trading port in the region up until the nineteenth century, exporting highly prized Black Isle grain, oats, bere (an early type of barley), wheat, linen, pigs, whisky and salted herring to London markets and across the North Sea to Baltic ports.

Rocky headlands, the Soutors of Cromarty, guard the approach to the harbour. "Soutor" is the old Scots word for shoemaker. Two giants, shoemakers, worked on the headlands and shared tools by tossing them to each other across the bay . . . so the story goes.

Cromarty captures the essential spirit of the Black Isle. Walking its narrow streets evokes a sense of timelessness; the old courthouse and gaol, with its distinctive clock tower; the Georgian symmetry of Cromarty House; the brewery building and fishermen's cottages; a Gaelic church, built to meet the religious needs of the Highland men and women who worked in Cromarty during the great years of the herring fishings. It is as though, in spite of "progress", nothing really has changed substantially. They are the same people, with the same hopes and aspirations as those who trod this way before.

Another place that evokes an enormous sense of peace is Fortrose Cathedral. My in-laws lived close by and when visiting them, I would recharge my spiritual batteries amidst the graceful sandstone ruins. A stone figure lies on top of the most important tomb on the grounds of the cathedral: Euphemia, Countess of Ross. Euphemia, after she was widowed in 1382, was married to Alexander Stewart, the illegitimate son of King Robert II, infamously known as "The Wolf of Badenoch".

Alex was much more interested in Euphemia's property than in acquiring a bride, and the minute he got what he wanted, he deserted Euphemia in favour of an accommodating mistress. The countess complained about her treatment to the Bishop of Moray, who threatened Alexander with excommunication. The Wolf decided to teach the Bishop a lesson and burned the Moray towns of Forres and Elgin, including Elgin Cathedral, adjudged to be the most beautiful cathedral in the civilised world. Euphemia is still waiting to reclaim her inheritance, while her "estranged" husband lies uneasily asleep in Dunkeld Cathedral, Perthshire.

The Jacobite Mackenzie Earls of Seaforth lie nearby. In 1880, a hoard of 1,100 silver coins was found, buried in the cathedral green. Could they have been part of the money sent from France in 1746 to Bonnie Prince Charlie and, allegedly, buried at the west end of Loch Arkaig to the north of Fort William?

The Black Isle holds golden memories for me and I always find it hard to leave. I have tramped its rocky shores and marveled at its flora and fauna for many years. There is in the Black Isle a sense of continuity, of order and permanence. It is as though no matter what the future might hold for my native land, this special corner of Scotland, with its wondrous woodlands and fertile fields, will forever remain true to itself, and to the people who call the Black Isle home.

43.
Of Guns, Rods and Gillies

The bedrock of a Scottish boy's life consists of rugby, gold and fishing. It is impossible to grow up in Scotland without becoming embroiled in these activities. I still hear, to this day, our school sportsmaster yelling at me, "Lie on the ball, Sandison, kill it!" Thus I learned the proper function of a fullback in an extreme emergency: to "kill" the ball when it is dangerously adjacent to the goal line whilst twenty-nine of my blood-crazed compatriots gathered round to kick the living daylights out of me.

Consequently, quickly developing a compelling interest in golf was easy. My father gave me four wooden-shafted clubs and a couple of grizzled balls, then let me loose on Swanston Golf Course in the Pentland Hills near Edinburgh. The smell of bacon and eggs cooking in the clubhouse kitchen on a cold morning is an enduring memory. As is the memory of the hours and hours I spent searching for these two, irreplaceable balls. Dad was notoriously short-tempered: "For God's sake, keep your eye on the ball, Bruce! It is the last one you will get from me."

So I decided to concentrate my mind on fishing and the great outdoors. It seemed to me to be the most sensible thing to do. No one else in my family fished, or hunted, or stalked the moors. Here, at least, I would be absolutely free to do my own thing and make my own mistakes well out of range of maniac rugby masters, prickly gorse bushes and outraged green-keepers. I acquired an old greenheart rod, an antiquated silk line, a small brass reel and a dozen tattered flies. Within a few weeks, I had taught myself how to cast and was off to the river.

That, I suppose, is the story of my life. I had discovered a joy that has comforted me for, well, decades. In the process, I also discovered my native land and its vibrant, often violent history. And I found Scotland's lonely places, amidst its blue-grey mountains and heather-covered moors. I learned to speak to statuesque red deer, rocketing grouse and cautious wildcat. My friends were playful otters, golden eagle and peregrine. I splashed and swam in remote summer-corrie lochans and saw sunsets and dawns that I will never forget.

Along the way, I also have had the pleasure of getting to know many of my fellow countrymen who care for and nurture Scotland's priceless natural heritage: the gillies, keepers and stalkers without whose hard work and dedication my native land would be a much poorer place. The Gaelic word "gille" means: a lad; a young man; servant man. The word has been corrupted in English usage as "gillie" but it means the same: a Highland chief's attendant, or the guide of hunting and fishing sportsmen. But it is "gillie" and never, ever "ghillie".

Myths and legends abound about the character, morals and humour of Scotland's gillies and, believe me, every single story is true; indeed, some are even truer. Their alleged love of whisky, *uisge beatha*, is well known, but in my time, I have met many more *uisge-beathaed* sportsmen than I have met under-the-weather gillies. The fact of the matter is that, like driving, whisky and looking after often-inexperienced guns or rods simply do not mix. The gillie needs a clear head in order to steer his guest out of trouble and to give him the best opportunity of sport.

Nevertheless, a decent dram is useful and sporting gentlemen in Scotland are well advised to carry a suitable supply. I was having such a dram one evening with a senior gillie when I asked him what was the worst thing that had ever happened to him during his time as a gillie. He paused, in the middle of a reflective sip, and considered my question: "Well, do you know, once I had a Gentleman out with me and after a while I realised that he had brought no whisky with him." As though still stunned by the memory, he was quiet for a few moments.

"What did you do?" I asked, shocked.

"Oh that was easy. I just took him to where there were no fish."

One of the most remarkable sporting sights in Scotland used to be the ballroom at Mar Lodge, near Balmoral on Deeside, which contained the heads of more than 2,000 stags. Tragically, the lodge was burned down some years ago and the ballroom destroyed. However, Donald MacDonald of Ballater, who was head keeper on the Invercauld Estate and whose father was a keeper at Mar, remembers being told about special deer drives when King George V used to come over from Balmoral for the occasion: "I have heard my father say that often twenty or thirty stags would be shot in a day, and I myself have seen as many as seventeen ponies going up the hill to collect them."

An Invercauld colleague of Donald's, Tom MacPhearson, told me about a day grouse shooting when he found the laird, Captain Farquharson, crouched on the floor of his butt, his jacket shredded as though it had been put through a mincer: "It's not safe, Tom," said the laird. "Some idiot is shooting at me, not at the damn birds." Tom worked with the laird the next day and soon found the culprit. It was a guest from China, in the neighboring butt, who was less than familiar with safety procedures and shooting etiquette.

As the grouse rocketed past the butts, Tom watched the Chinese guest. His loaded gun swung round to the left, following the flight of the incoming birds far beyond the safety point and in line with the laird's butt. Tom yelled a warning as the Chinaman's gun blasted shot in their direction and he and the laird flopped to the floor. Tom accosted the culprit: "Now, Sir," Tom said, "that was very nearly your best shot of the day – the laird and his head keeper with one barrel!"

The late Jock McAskill of Invergarry, in the Great Glen, was another expert stalker. Three generations of McAskills worked at Invergarry, starting before the First World War with Jock's grandfather. Jock began his stalking career on the Brae Roy Estate in Glen Roy, where the head keeper was getting on in years and his eyesight beginning to fail. On the first morning on the hill, he said to Jock: "Now then, lad, just give me a good nudge if you see anything." Jock was also an expert angler, his last great expedition being when he took four salmon in a morning from Loch Oich, the heaviest of which weighed 17lbs.

One of the most famous angling developments in the middle years of the century was that of greased line fishing for salmon, invented on the River Dee at Cairnton by legendary angler Arthur Wood. Wood claimed great success fishing for salmon in low water conditions by using a line that floated on the surface of the water, rather than using a sinking line that "swims" below the surface. His most successful pattern of salmon fly, he alleged, was a small pattern called the Blue Charm and every angling magazine in Britain was full of the story.

However, Jimmy Ross of Rothes told me a different story. As a young man, Jimmy used to gillie at Aboyne on the Dee and knew Arthur Wood's gillie. In the pub one night, Jimmy plied his colleague with drams and quizzed him about all these fish supposedly being killed on a wee Blue Charm fished by Arthur Wood on a floating line. "Don't you believe it!" replied Wood's gillie. "It's a great big Jock Scott on a sinking line that he is doing all the damage, and everybody for miles around lashing away with wee Blue Charms catching nothing!"

David Hanton was one of Scotland's most respected keepers. The Hanton family served the Cortachy Castle Estate in Angus for many years. David's grandfather was head keeper for nearly sixty years and two of his sons worked for the estate. David's own father had been head keeper and David himself worked on the estate all his life, on the moor and as a gillie on the River South Esk.

When I first met David, he had been retired for several years but he was still as bright and spry as a spring morning. A coal fire burned in the grate and the living room was scattered with the memorabilia of a lifetime spent out of doors. With a twinkle in his eye, he complained to me: "Do you know, when I was a boy of seventeen, I joined the Gordon Highlanders and I can remember it as clearly as though it were yesterday. Now, last week I put away two spools of fishing nylon and I'm damned if I can remember where I put them."

David began fishing in Glen Clova, one of the five glorious glens of Angus, in the Burn of Heughs by the side of his grandfather's house: "What a grand place for a young lad! There was a stream in front of the lodge, which came down from Ben Tirram, and it had fine pools with a trout under every stone." David was injured on Vimy Ridge during the First World War and he told me: "I was hit by a whiz-bang . . . it was like being hit by the side of a house. As I fell to the ground, I remember thinking, 'well, that's the end of your keepering days, my lad,' but I recovered and I have been a keeper ever since."

Another well-loved South Esk gillie was Ned Coates, who started his keepering days with Big Bill Robertson, a farmer and potato merchant and owner of the House of Dunn: "Noo, Ned, whit wages do you get?" asked Robertson of the young man seeking employment. "Ten pounds a week," Ned replied. "Well, I'll gie ye the same, with free milk, free tatties and a free house. Dinna call me Bill or Sir. Just call me Boss." Ned has never owned a pair of trousers in his life and always wears the kilt. "It's a bit sharp in the spring, wading out to land a fish, but the kilt just floats up around me and soon dries out again afterwards."

Today, on moor, loch, river and hill, I am constantly surprised by just how young Scotland's gillies are. And as the seasons pass, they seem to get even younger, year by year. This is a great mystery to me because I have stayed the same age, from the time I lay in the mud on that rugby field until the present day. I have not changed one iota. I believe I owe this attitude to the happy days I spend amidst the cathedral-like wilderness of the land I love, and to the excellent company of the kindest and most courteous breed of men that I have ever met, Scotland's gillies.